The American Paradox

By Helene S. Zahler

THE AMERICAN PARADOX
EASTERN WORKINGMEN AND NATIONAL LAND POLICY

with Louis M. Hacker

THE UNITED STATES IN THE TWENTIETH CENTURY

THE AMERICAN
PARADOX

by Helene S. Zahler

Foreword by Louis M. Hacker,
Professor of Economics, Columbia University

New York   E. P. DUTTON & CO., INC.   1964

Published simultaneously in Canada by Clark, Irwin &
Company Limited, Toronto and Vancouver

Library of Congress Catalog Card Number: 64-11084

To E. Louise Mally

ACKNOWLEDGMENTS

I wish to express my deep appreciation to Dr. Hendrik Ruitenbeek, who urged that this book should be written, and to E. Louise Mally, who helped so immeasurably in bringing it into being. I should also like to mention the unfailingly gracious assistance of Columbia University Library's reference staff and the patient cooperation of Miss Muriel Fleischman who, in typing this book, brought order into a difficult manuscript.

Contents

Foreword

ALL THOSE who are interested in and fascinated by the American experience, which is made up of so many polarities, will want to read Helene S. Zahler's new, thoughtful, and at the same time troubled interpretation. She will receive the hearing that is her due: a close and trained student of American history, keenly alert to the varying winds of doctrine, yet swept away by none of them, Miss Zahler is both judicious and bold. The factual materials of her essay stand up under close scrutiny; the molds into which she has cast them—the relations of the American to his world and to himself—constitute part of that greater examination in which many intelligent persons like herself are engaging today.

Miss Zahler calls her book *The American Paradox*. She is aware, nevertheless, that there are many, perhaps even an infinite number, of paradoxes and they take the forms of both rejection and reception. The American settlers fled from the unequal institutions of Europe—the closed, stratified societies of prescription and class—and yet brought with them Calvinism, the English Rule of Law, and John Locke. They accepted, inevitably, democracy, which, that prescient young French visitor Tocqueville saw, meant majority rule and egalitarianism; the other side of the coin—the paradox—was the obligation to preserve minority and

individual rights. They made heroes of the striving and competitive industrial entrepreneurs; and in another generation
had turned them into anti-heroes.

The Old World, West and East, particularly to the first
generation native-born American, was alien; the second
and third proceeded to sink their roots deep in the whole
heritage of man. We were out of Europe and yet part of
the Atlantic Community; we had gone our separate ways—
more committed to the whole ranging sweep of individual
right and private decision than any other previous culture—
and yet realized that our survival depended upon the
strength and unity of the free world. Liberty, apparently,
as long as it left untouched the integrity of men, had many
forms.

To Miss Zahler, the contemporary American—"lonely,
anxious, alienated, conformist"—is the product of the world
he created; it is in his process of growth and change that
such characteristics were formed. But are they more than
caught in a moment of time? The pulling and tugging of
both wanting to belong and seeking to be free have been the
conditions of life in which all Americans have grown up.

Miss Zahler points out justly that the English mainland
colonists sought to remain a part of the world they had
left behind; this was the fear from the start of loneliness
and alienation. The Europe they had come from was a
corporate world—of church, chartered cities with their free-
men and freedoms, guilds, organized villages. They quickly
saw this meant privilege and prescription, whether of a
theocratic state or limitations upon access to property. The
struggle against authority—that grace was to be achieved
only in the company of the elect; that property was to exist

only in its corporate form—almost at once became normative.

How could it be otherwise in a wide, open, unpopulated
land where release from the limitations and restraints of
prescription was just over the hill or a stretch down the
coast or up a river? By so doing—in the process forming an
independent church, staking out a clearing (the land was
paid for later under squatter's rights), setting up a new
town—loneliness and alienation were price and challenge.
Miss Zahler puts the initial paradox in religious terms: "The
first Puritan generation had been a frontier people, physically isolated, standing alone with a wrathful God whom
they had come to the wilderness to serve."

And then, as part of the drama of escape and survival—
in the creation of new communities and of a firm sense of
achievement and belonging—the "people who lived on the
frontier experienced the psychological impact of the contradiction between the faith [of Calvinism] which said man
is a creature without power to act to save his soul and the
demands of an environment which made intense effort the
condition of his existence." The round was unending: alienation, conformity, alienation. The status of freedom
demands the first; those who find the race too harsh seek
shelter in the second. But as they try to press their standards
of taste and behavior on the whole of society, there are
always nonconformists who will break away.

Perhaps alienation is a price we pay for freedom. The
creative artist has always sensed this. The minority which
establishes its own community, and, in the modern jargon,
its own infrastructures—whether they were the Irish of
the nineteenth century, the Jews of the early twentieth,
the contemporary Puerto Ricans of New York, or the

Mexicans of California and the Southwest—closes ranks to escape the bitterness of being outsiders and unwanted; and in the process new conformities appear. The communities dissolve when the individual has found strength in this common purpose—and he steps out once more unafraid but alone.

This is the American paradox: and the end result of the American experience—that institutions and individuals are constantly in a state of becoming, that values are not what the facts say they are but what they ought to be.

Miss Zahler seems to think it was somewhat easier in the eighteenth and nineteenth centuries, when she compares Jonathan Edwards with Ralph Waldo Emerson in a striking passage—one of the many in her book.

> For Edwards, true religion required a respect for the majesty of God great enough to accept, if not welcome one's own damnation. For Emerson, true religion required a respect for the majesty of the human soul too great to allow it to depend on any inherited mode of belief or any customary form of observance. . . . The two views have in common the insistence that each man, for himself, accept responsibility for deciding whether he could claim conviction that he was saved. . . . Both called on men to live in the company of loneliness, but the loneliness they contemplated did not involve the modern sense of separation from self.

It is this last that worries her most as she looks about her. Alienation has developed between people by "the increasing competitive pressures of life" in an industrialized, corporate, impersonal society. There is indifference to "larger questions in politics and general reluctance to recognize and attack social problems." We have settled our own wilderness; but the larger contemporary wilderness is the post-atomic world. "Yet faith in the potential importance of individual action as a means of saving oneself and others from the real hell which can open beneath us is hard for the contemporary person to maintain."

Nevertheless, the climate for remaining free is still here, more real in fact than possibly anywhere else. Those of us who are aware how much more complex the business of living has become, and by the same token also aware of the deep necessity for keeping the ways of escape open—for minorities and hence for the individual; in the present-day struggle, for example, for civil rights because it is part of the greater effort always to preserve civil liberties—must accept Miss Zahler's statement, as she means it, as challenge. It is a good and reflective statement, even if it is, as I started out by saying, a troubled one.

LOUIS M. HACKER

Columbia University
June 3, 1964

The American Paradox

Introduction   1

FOREIGN OBSERVERS, who are apt to see in the United
States what Americans merely take for granted, have long
been aware of America as a paradox. Whether the observer
came hopefully or prepared to disapprove, his attention
has been caught by the divergence between the practice of
life in America and the premises upon which Americans
say their lives and society are based. The divergence between the visible performance and the principles upon
which action is said to rest constitutes what this book calls
paradox. The distance between aspiration and actuality cannot be measured, to be sure, but what can be observed in
this area is none the less significant for helping us understand the distresses which affect and afflict current American life.

The modern American is a lonely person, alienated from
society and his fellows, anxious about himself, his relations
with others, the world he lives in; a gregarious person, uneasy when alone, so little able to endure silence or himself
that he must have background music wherever he goes; a
proclaimed individualist who exerts himself to be as like all
the other proclaimed individualists as his purse allows. The
American is so certain that he is leading the best of all possible lives that he supports an uncounted number of physi-

cians of the soul and makes books on peace of mind and
peace of soul into best sellers. The American cherishes his
independence of mind by huddling into the coziness of mass
media. He preens himself as the average middle-class man
with no pretentions to be better or wiser than his fellows
and shudders at the inevitable mediocrity of collectivist
societies. He praises responsible government and uses "politician" as a term of abuse. He believes in due process of
law and has made the vigilante a folk hero. He proclaims
that "money isn't everything" and works himself into ulcers
in the effort to get more.

Lonely, anxious, alienated, conformist—so the American
is described. Some observers cast the description in terms
that imply a past in which these distresses did not afflict him.
But when one goes in search of that happy past, it recedes
generation by generation until one knows that, to those who
lived in it, no age was golden.

The historical roots of the American characteristics just
sketched will be the subject of this book. For undoubtedly
our current distresses and problems have not been shaped
merely by the strains of contemporary life. Other nations
faced with nearly identical current stresses respond in very
different ways. It is obvious, therefore, that we need to explore the past in order to discover the pattern in which the
fabric of our current life and its problems has been woven.

The person alone, without stake in his world, is familiar
to contemporary psychologists. His suffering or his defiance
of suffering runs through many a contemporary novel.
Loneliness is not peculiar to America, of course, but the
conditions of the American past have given it a peculiar,
almost a poignant quality. For those conditions have tended
to give many people a sense of guilt about feeling lonely:

men were supposed to be strong and strength meant self-sufficiency. Yet loneliness was a pervasive part of American existence. Sometimes the American's loneliness came from an enforced, yet self-chosen distance from his kind. Sometimes the American's loneliness was a burden greater than living separated from others in the wilderness; rather it was the empty darkness of life without true fellowship, although in small towns and settlements one's neighbors are close and keeping watch.

That watchfulness may have bred and fostered conformity, although pressure for conformity in externals was no American peculiarity. Certainly, loneliness fostered anxiety and it might often bear witness to alienation as well.

The alienated man is rootless, without ties to his work or his fellows, sometimes apparently without ties to, or knowledge of, himself. The psychological and sociological meaning of alienation in our society might well be dealt with at length from those specialized points of view. But the peculiar experience of American man has given alienation in the United States its distinctive quality.

The British colonies on mainland North America were the first place to which large numbers of European families came to make permanent homes and establish a society less in the image of what they had left than in the image of their own desire. To be sure, the people who settled what is now the United States could leave their past behind them no more than could those who came afterward. Yet their very migration did represent some desire to do that. One need not agree completely with Geoffrey Gorer, declaring that American society represents a repudiation of the father, to recognize the basic element of alienation in the willingness to leave the parent community—not to reproduce it, as did the colonies of the ancient Greek cities; rather to make it over and find in the new community the place which the old had denied the immigrant.

If one looks at nineteenth-century American heroes, folk, fictional, and political, they are seen as men without family, sons who raise their hands against their fathers and go off to seek lives elsewhere. If one looks at American facts, one sees the myth re-enacted on another stage. During the decades between 1830 and 1910, the years of the great migration from Europe, it was the rejected who crossed the ocean—not the comfortable and accepted, but those who felt themselves unwanted and without place.

The United States summoned one kind of alienated man, then, and the conditions of life for the immigrant tended to alienate men further. If the immigrant lived in ghettoes, as so often he did, his children lived in limbo, cut off from parents and their past, yet freed only to live on the fringes of the majority community.

But the anxious feelings and anxiously conforming behavior of many immigrants' children, the people once contemptuously labeled "the hyphenates," does not mean that the source of alienation in America is to be found in the experience of its so-called new immigrants alone. Nor is alienation only the product of swift industrialization on a massive scale. Alienation is part of an older American tradition, and that tradition is linked to a more ancient Western concept of the man divided, seeking to have reason govern passion, spirit rule body, and finding explanation for his repeated failures in elaborate mythologies about the nature of man. The Puritan who felt he could do no good but must not do evil is brother to the recent immigrant's child who felt that he could not be accepted in the native community, yet could not comfortably relapse into his parents' ways of life.

The kind of loneliness which the twentieth-century American experiences as being alone in a hostile or indifferent world is not too unlike the feelings of the seventeenth-century migrant who stood alone with his prospect of damnation and turned to another world to find his friend. As that kind of faith diminished, men became more aware of their isolation. This awareness afflicted the artist and the intellectual particularly and finally became the theme of that strand in our literature which has been called "the revolt from the village." The frontier was passing away by the time this theme emerged into literature; broad emptiness had given way to town and incipient city. Yet well before the theme achieved mature literary expression, one can see alienation expressed in two viewpoints: "The American community is unfit for the sensitive man to live in"; and "The man who is troubled by what doesn't trouble me isn't fit to live in the American community."

The second viewpoint creates our conventional image of conformity as the first has created our conventional image of alienation. Men sought refuge from the fear of loneliness and the pain of alienation by doing as their neighbors did. When liberty was defined as liberty to do what was right, and right was understood as that which one's neighbor approved, a man was most free when he conformed most closely. As we shall see, freedom to obey was considered true civil liberty in the seventeenth century. With time, liberty became freedom to do as the next man did. Finally, in our own day, the fellow man from whom one was estranged and alienated by the context of a changing economic life, by the maturing of an urbanized impersonal social organization, and by the difficulty of truly human

communication became the source at once of one's comfort
and one's distress.

Yet enforced and empty conformity tended to generate
a deeper degree of alienation, particularly among intellectuals. Nor could conformity long offer adequate protection
against anxiety. It is for the psychologist to examine
anxiety and its consequences in depth. Here we are not
concerned with the basic anxiety that expresses the panic
generated by being restrained of one's natural impulses and
forced to accept civilization and its curbs. Rather, we are
interested in the consequences of what was at least the implicit demand that all Americans live by what many felt to
be a contradictory set of principles. One set of these may
be stated as the idea that in and of himself man could do
nothing to save his soul, and that gaining the world confers
no profit. Upon this basis, modified in ways that will be
shown in subsequent chapters, the United States was
founded.

If men behaved as the logic of their convictions would
seem to require, those who accepted the doctrine of man's
spiritual impotence should have been passive and fatalistic
people who turned their energies toward the inner life.
Instead, and in accelerating measure, Americans became a
people who might be characterized by the wartime slogan
of their navy's construction battalions: "The difficult we do
right away; the impossible takes a little longer." In the
centuries since 1630, the United States has followed a second set of principles, embodied in the conviction that he
who strives shall gain the world and save his soul in the gaining.

Contradiction is thus evident in the pattern of American
growth, and contradiction expresses and is expressed in

conflict. The paradoxical elements of the American character—assuming that such an entity exists—are an outgrowth and reflection of American experience. This experience has developed in the intellectual context of the system of beliefs which our Puritan ancestors erected upon the already paradoxical foundation which Calvin laid. As will be brought out in more detail later, we may justifiably talk of our Puritan ancestors because many of the beliefs of the intellectual leaders of the Massachusetts Bay colonists were shared by their counterparts in other colonies and also because their efforts at imparting those beliefs created the social climate in which the essential paradox developed.

To put it briefly, and therefore somewhat crudely, the country which was to become the United States was founded—so far as its intellectual life was concerned—by highly articulate and self-conscious people who accepted Calvin's doctrine that man was radically corrupt and that God was wholly sovereign. God showed his absolute sovereignty, Calvin argued, by determining that some men should be saved and other men be damned. However it might be hedged and qualified, this doctrine was essentially fatalistic and arbitrary.

Particularly during the two generations after the publication of the French version of the *Institutes*, some of Calvin's followers in England and elsewhere modified the doctrine in order to accommodate the effort which they recognized as necessary for man's moral life and for the economic development of his society. Yet Calvin's English followers continued to assert that they had not departed from his philosophy. Historically, we are thus faced with the contradiction in which it is altogether possible that many of the paradoxical aspects of modern American life have their roots.

It certainly seems remarkable to declare that a being who is impotent to do good should be required to behave well. When this being is declared to be not only impotent but also destined to a rather probable damnation, to demand moral conduct from him seems even more paradoxical. The Englishmen who modified what they apparently recognized as Calvin's dangerously fatalistic doctrine employed a set of rationalizations which supplied a further source of contradiction. These, too, are matters which will be discussed more fully as the ramifications of the paradox are explored.

For one set of paradoxes gave rise to others, and maintaining beliefs in apparent contradiction generated a high degree of psychological tension. In many respects, belief in man's spiritual helplessness continued to exert influence in the eighteenth and nineteenth centuries. Yet by the mid-nineteenth century, action had become a cult in the United States; individual responsibility developed into a shibboleth ultimately vulgarized in the "rags to riches" legend.

Other people who had embraced creeds declaring "all is written" also experienced outbursts of energy. But Islam's conquering élan dimmed in a few generations, and lethargy settled over the people who once had been not merely conquerors but mediators between a creative East and a still crudely receptive West, between the lost world of Greece and medieval Atlantic Europe.

Accelerating energy is not a necessary outcome of belief that each man's fate is determined. Nevertheless, as A. L. Rowse has observed, determinist beliefs on any level, religious or secular, often free their followers for enterprises which seem laden with risk to those who do not so believe.

Since God, or history, has decided the long-term outcome in favor of one's cause, present action becomes at once more of an obligation and less of a threat.

However one accounts for the emergence of cults of action from philosophies of determinism, even a hurried scanning of the record shows that belief in predestination did not paralyze Calvinist energies in Europe. When England's Puritans wrought the changes in Calvinism which will be described in the next chapter, the energy level rose still higher, until striving became a prime end of man. Effort, moreover, was accompanied by an obligation to accept responsibility which also seems paradoxical. For once again, consistency would seem to suggest, if not to dictate, irresponsibility to a person whose soul's fate has already been decided. Why, for example, need any man be morally concerned with his present good behavior if he has been damned since the world began? Or, if his salvation has been decreed, why need he concern himself with conduct, since that could win him only the second-rate rewards which earthly life was supposed to offer? If conduct were taken as evidence, incentive to moral effort might become greater, to be sure. But Calvin's doctrine did not state that good works were a certain sign of salvation nor even that evil conduct inevitably pointed to damnation.

Calvin and his fellow preachers were so aware of the social peril of their doctrine that they held the full truth to be matter only for the select few who would not be tempted to irresponsibility by the knowledge of God's arbitrary power and indisputable justice. Later, however, good conduct did indeed become a sign. Men then considered it a token of grace if they were able to keep God's commandments truly, at least much of the time.

A man did good to others then, not as he wished to be done by on earth and beyond, but rather to show his faith and the grace that made it possible for him to have faith. Even a man certain that he was damned might accept responsibility to behave well. For sinful man should glorify his sovereign God by effort at obedience even if that sovereignty required his own damnation. To be sure, we have few if any records of those who were "notable saints" in behavior who long cherished the disquieting conviction that they might be damned. Rather, as we shall see, belief that one was destined to perdition soon was recognized as a temptation of the devil. And yet that terrified belief lingered.

Accepting responsibility for one's behavior is linked with another aspect of the basic American paradox, the tension between desire to enjoy a foredestined salvation in eternity and desire for material success in time. These apparently contradictory objectives also were reconciled in developing Calvinism. Those who have gathered the spiritual riches of well-doing may find themselves rewarded with more tangible riches. By the late seventeenth century, in spite of hesitations and warnings, he who prospered was often considered saved.

Once again, out of a system of belief which mere consistency would pursue into otherworldliness and indifference to material gain came a people all but dedicated to the opinion that business was the only proper business of man. Very soon, Americans lived not as if this world were a proving ground of one's fitness for future bliss, but as if this were the only world.

Yet in this world, Americans lived in the future tense; they came to exemplify particularly the man who "never is, but always to be blessed." In a society like that of nine-teenth-century America, where striving itself seemed the most valued virtue, many men endured the present for the future's sake. That future they saw vividly enough to make their lives' present deficiencies fade from their awareness. To cite a specific observer, Charles Dickens, mud and ague were the present reality of the American West in the 1830's. The cities which he saw so splendidly drawn in real-estate offices were either promoters' frauds or expressions of ex-aggerated expectations like the dusty magnificent distances and unfinished Capitol at Washington.

Long after Dickens' *American Notes* described a per-ished world, those who eyed American culture from out-side noted how this ground was continually being prepared for a cultural flowering that was continually on the very verge of happening.

To move from concern for a future invisible, because it lay in a reality beyond time, to concern for a future un-seen, because it lay in an earthly time to come, is not too startling a shift of focus. The change becomes even less sur-prising, perhaps, when one recalls another shift: the singu-lar metamorphosis by which concentration on the rewards of this world grew out of concentrated attention to one's prospects in the world beyond.

Belief that God chose some to be saved while others were damned generated another set of paradoxes than those just surveyed. These were concerned with political philoso-phy rather than with the larger issue of what treasure men sought and where they meant to lay it up.

Those chosen to be saved surely should constitute an aristocracy. And, as we shall see, the leaders of the Puritan group organized both secular and church government in a fashion intended to establish and preserve rule by the best, that is, the Lord's probable elect. Nevertheless, the American rather soon became notable, or notorious if one prefers, for his reluctance to recognize his "betters." Heroes he might worship, to be sure, but if one observes these heroes, particularly in the nineteenth century, they seem to display more sharply and on a larger scale the qualities which men of smaller achievement felt at least latently present in themselves. The aggressive independence of Andrew Jackson, the humane shrewdness of Lincoln, the energy and skill of Carnegie—these were characteristics which the American could admire without regarding their possessors as of a different kind from himself. All had fought to rise, and all had won. None had been originally favored by society; all had shown that men were equal and that the potentialities of such equal men were high.

Yet this kind of hero and the concept of democratic equality itself developed in a society which, in its early period, in the seventeenth century, abhorred the very word "democracy." To be sure, one might contend that the idea of all men as equal was in accord with the doctrine that man could not help himself, for both Calvin and those who built their doctrine on his agreed that, since no man was spared damnation because he was worthy of being saved, merely as men even the elect were no better than the reprobate.

A paradox, too, may be found in the role which God's absolute sovereignty played in the post-Calvinist scheme of salvation. God's will was law, except as He Himself chose to limit that will by promises freely given (and fully binding). And those who believed in so absolutely sovereign a God in heaven might be expected to bow before a matching absolutism on earth. Truly, those who accepted the absolute majesty of God did tend to believe that the magistrates who represented some of God's functions should have special respect and obedience from the people they governed. Yet not only in what was to become the United States, but in the Netherlands, in Scotland, in Geneva, and in England, those who believed in the absolute sovereignty of God also tended to believe that the power of magistrates should be strictly bridled.

For magistrates operated governments, and governments were a necessary consequence of the corruption of man's nature. Although the Puritan group regarded government as necessary and indeed saw God's order in the physical universe echoed in the order of rank and station on earth, they could not fully purify human government of its origins. Since government was made necessary by evil, government came to be considered evil in itself. Furthermore, government must have power, and men, being what they were, all too readily exploited power for evil purposes.

Thus, those who accepted an absolutely sovereign God did not transfer that kind of sovereignty to earth; rather they rejected absolute kings (perhaps as encroaching on divinity) and finally came to insist that government itself—not merely governing persons—also be limited. If all that a tyrant could abuse—property, freedom of movement, liberty of expression—were protected against governmental intrusion, the rewards of tyranny might seem less tempting. And this, as will become clear later, developed into the basic constitutional theory of the United States.

The country whose first intellectual leaders elaborated and rationalized the paradoxes we have been dealing with produced a true complexity of paradoxes as it grew. Men's equality in deserving damnation, the root and branch cor-

ruption of men's nature, was transmuted into an equality
of noble potential as the eighteenth century advanced. Even
the seventeenth-century leaders admitted that the being who
was radically corrupt had, after all, been created in the
image of perfection and that traces of what man once was
lingered with him always.

Thus, man might be thought of as a lofty as well as a
fallen creature. Nevertheless, even an essentially noble man
could not quite be trusted: what fell from glory in Eden
was all too likely to lapse from virtue on earth. Americans
of the nineteenth century watched their neighbors as cen-
soriously when they said they believed in man's goodness
as their forefathers had kept watch over their neighbors
when they said they believed in universal depravity.

Between 1630 and 1776, however, man who was wicked
came to be considered fit to be free, but he still could not be
trusted with the edged tools of freedom. Once Americans
had said, with John Cotton, that persecution of evil notions
was no persecution at all. Yet those who later most loudly
proclaimed their faith in the intellectual market place,
which purified all things including ideas, were often most
ready to bar it to all opinions but their own. In 1961, for
example, the radical right and the radical left achieved complete accord: each agreed that the other should not be allowed to present its opinions to the untoughened mind of
the college student (but the right was quixotic enough to be
willing to be banned itself in order to keep its enemy silent).

We have observed that Americans transformed universal depravity, and therefore worthlessness, into an almost universal worth: they moved from "all men are bad"
to "men like me are probably more good than evil." The
movement to "most men are like me" was long in coming.

Indeed, democratic equality was transformed into a peculiarly virulent version of the aristocracy of race. Those who had little but the color of their skins to bless themselves with proclaimed their equality with the mighty by finding inferiors to kick. Racism as bolster to equality was not entirely American, to be sure, nor did racism reach its direst flowering in the United States. Nevertheless, in this country during the decades before the Civil War, the defenders of slavery proclaimed that the presence of enslaved Negroes made all white men equal. Thus, they argued, Southern society was unified in a way impossible in the North where possessions divided men.

Whether man was a noble being or a corrupt creature in need of watching, whether he was oriented toward material acquisition or toward generosity in disposing of his material gains, post-Calvinist thinkers agreed that man had to act. And American man acting tended to make action itself his characteristic purpose. Increasingly, however, the complicated economy which effort had helped to create made irrelevant the kind of daring effort which had created it. The growing complexity of the economy made individuals seem less significant, increasingly expendable, more easily replaceable one by another—if not by ingeniously punched tapes activating ingenious machinery.

Slowly, the paradox shifts. Apparently, Americans have made a group commitment to effort. Yet increasingly in the twentieth century they tend to find effort of the traditional risky sort too painful for what they see as its potential reward. By the 1950's, students of society were recording young men more interested in the retirement pensions offered by prospective employers than in the level of present salaries or in future chances of achieving wealth. These young men may have been precisely the exceptions which test all rules. Or they may have had a keen eye for actuality.

And thus the paradox continues. We shall follow the American through what appears to be a spiraling pattern of development. The Puritan sense of spiritual impotence will be transformed into an imperative for worldly success. Submission to God will turn into submission to an impersonal market which will, in turn, be transformed and personified until in the late nineteenth century the market will be talked of as if it were a just and beneficent though inexorable deity. In the mid-twentieth century, as we shall see, submission to the market is transforming itself, if some sociologists are accurate in their analysis, into submission to a peer group, directionless as the market and potentially wrathful, exacting its penalties and bestowing its rewards, not in the next world but in this. A people who set out believing that this world was a way station and a place of trial for the future now say they believe this is the best of all possible worlds. To be sure, it is still experienced as a place of testing; men test themselves against others in anxious, lonely search for status and identity. But men recognize their enemies as other men, or, if they are more sophisticated, they recognize their enemy as within themselves. And some men search for a self they seem unable to find.

The doctrine of the corruption of human nature seems to have been forgotten, as an operational fact; and eternity has been left to shift for itself while Americans—having joined churches in numbers that make them statistically more concerned with salvation than they have ever been— try to preserve themselves in an all too problematical time.

Old World Baggage 2

THE MODERN WORLD begins in the seventeenth century, some historians tell us. And they measure modernity by the degree to which well-educated people have put scientific understanding in the place of religious images of the structure and operation of the universe. If we accept that interpretation, the United States, although first settled in the seventeenth century, began its existence in the later medieval world. Its intellectual leaders accepted Copernicus' picture of the solar system, but they did not take for granted the basic assumption of science: general laws can be seen to govern the universe and to act without regard for the needs and desires of men. By knowledge of such laws, men may make themselves more comfortable, wealthier, even more powerful, but the laws operate of themselves; they need no authorization from God and they show no concern for man.

In seventeenth-century New England, general law operated, but only by God's permission and within the framework of His sovereignty. No one in New England's founding generation doubted that man was the vital center of God's universe. And New England had far more in common with the other colonies than one generally realizes. To those who thought about anything beyond their workaday world, man and his soul were of eternal significance. Against the burden of eternity, what occurred in time could be of no real importance. Yet man lived in time, and in time, somehow, he must work through his life to his fore-destined end, saved or among the damned.

In this situation, one aspect of the American paradox has its roots. Because man's salvation had to be made manifest in time, time tended to oust eternity from the center of men's attention. Americans paid lip service to eternity—first to eternal salvation, then to ethical principles of eternal validity; now they render tribute to the comfortable vagueness of "values"—and Americans have always believed their service to be sincere. Yet time, and time's profit, have grown in importance until the testimony which time afforded—notably material success itself—has become a kind of eternal value.

A few decades ago, even with the First World War behind them, historians had to exert sophisticated imaginations in order to feel the reality of a period in which men gave the last days first claim on their attention and their concern. Currently, many men in many ways are trying to divert their attention from the threatened approach of days that will be no less the last because they threaten the extermination of a species rather than the torment of individual souls.

Twentieth-century Americans faced with this threat feel restive and even resentful in a situation that requires them to take responsible political action when the prospect of making such action count seems to be slight. Their seventeenth-century predecessors acquired and even exacerbated a conviction of responsibility although being helpless was a tenet of their faith. Today's American and his forerunners have anxiety in common, then, and, when examined, the sources of their anxiety also have something in common although one is medieval and the other surely modern.

When Edmund Burke urged Parliament to take the cash of commercial advantage and let the credit of formal dominance go, he warned his colleagues that they were dealing with the "dissidence of dissent" and the "protestantism of the Protestant religion." The Puritan ancestors of the people Burke was discussing rejected the label of dissenter: they knew the truth; it was their opponents who dissented from it.

The Reformation was that split within Christendom whereby part of Europe rejected the supremacy of the Pope, claimed the Bible translated into the vernacular as the source of all valid religious authority, and embraced various doctrines different in some degree from the major doctrines of Rome. By and large, it also rejected the formalism, the pomp, ceremony, and drama of the mass. To the English Puritans, the Anglican stress on liturgical order and stately decorum in worship smelled of incense and decay. To them, its bishops and archbishops resembled the Roman apparatus which reform should have cast out of England's religion. Anglican doctrine, for all that it could be made to bear a Calvinist interpretation, left too many openings for the inventions of man and, particularly, for the assertion that he had some independent ability to save his soul.

As seen by Reformation theology, man was corrupt by nature. This belief was neither new nor Christian. Precursors of Christianity and early Christian heretics alike shared the belief that pure spirit had somehow mingled itself with matter and produced the corrupt being which was man. Time itself must pass away before what should not have been joined was finally separated and the universe thus became perfect once again.

Christianity agreed that man's nature was tainted. But orthodox Christianity rejected extremes of that belief. Over the centuries, the Catholic Church had elaborated systems of doctrine and of rite, for the intellectual to understand as he obeyed and for the ordinary man to practice without question; fallen man in his corruption retained sufficient goodness to be able to use and profit from the means of grace which a just and merciful God had provided.

The Protestant reformers regarded man's corruption less indulgently. Man was of such a nature that he could use and profit from the means of grace only if God extended him special favor.

In their view of human nature, the Reformation theologians turned back to Augustine, to what they considered the earliest and therefore the most pure Christian doctrine. Their opponents in the Roman Church did not deny the validity of what the Reformers called primitive doctrine; it was the emphasis of the Reformers (as well as their disobedience to authority) which was held to be in grievous error.

As everyone knows, political and economic conflicts in the sixteenth and seventeenth centuries expressed themselves in terms of theological differences. It has been argued that Luther succeeded where John Huss, the fourteenth-century Bohemian theologian,[1] had failed, rather largely because

[1] He was inspired to attack abuses in the Church by the influence of an earlier, English reformer, John Wycliffe. Huss was persuaded to come and defend his views at the Council of Constance, but while there he was treacherously seized, tried, condemned as a heretic, and burned. His followers carried on a prolonged civil war, animated both by nationalist Czech aims and by a desire for religious and social reform, but they were finally defeated in 1436.

Luther could appeal to German merchants and princes who had had a century longer in which to develop resentment against what they considered exploitation by churchmen from beyond the mountains. Italian churchmen controlled the means of grace and exacted payment for them. The Reform—as the Protestant movement often called itself—had most durable success in those parts of Europe which were both far from Rome and in the process of economic growth. And the Reform contended that grace was given, not in any way procured, and that man was saved by faith, not works.

Whatever may be the historians' current view of the argument that the Reformation expressed the desire of merchants and manufacturers to be free of religious impediments to profit-making—and these included both the belief that taking interest on money was wrong and the belief that, since all goods had a just price, no religious man should seek to get more—it is evident that, as heresy had flourished along the routes of commerce in the Middle Ages, so the Reform flourished among merchants and townsmen, whether in the Germanies, in France, or farther north.

In the late 1300's, Englishmen had been somewhat responsive to the heresy of John Wycliffe and the Lollards, with its emphasis on lay access to the Bible and its denial of magic efficacy to the sacraments, but although responsiveness did go as far as a small armed revolt in 1401, it had not withstood persecution. (Whether some followers of Wycliffe did "go underground" with their English Bibles is disputed by historians. Whether Wycliffe's ideas affected English reformers in the next generation is equally a matter for scholarly contention.) Englishmen in those generations held their religious convictions with a certain easiness of spirit. The national genius for compromise had long since reconciled English Christianity and the English world, and that genius made itself evident during the early phase of the English Reformation. Relative indifference to the fate of what had long seemed rather a foreign institution made it possible for Henry VIII to defend the Roman Catholic faith against Luther in 1521 and, in 1534, declare himself head of the Church of England without rousing much popular resistance. The British historian, F. M. Powicke, observes dryly that Englishmen knew about the new learning and the new theology, but though humanism or Luther might stir their minds, wholesome indifference to ideas kept those minds from becoming too unsettled.[2]

Nevertheless, as the Reformation took root in England, this indifference to ideology tended to diminish. When Henry was succeeded by his son, the English Church became more Protestant. When Catholic Mary Tudor succeeded her Protestant brother on the throne and tried to restore the Old Religion, many earnest Protestants had to choose between martyrdom and migration. Residence in Protestant centers on the Continent tended to strengthen English interest in ideas and particularly in the ideas of John Calvin. The Geneva reformer set forth his ideas in a systematic theology, as Luther did not; those ideas emphasized man's helplessness in the grip of his corruption—a doctrine Luther shared. Yet all men would not be damned, though all deserved to be, for it was God's sovereign will that some be saved. That will, and that alone, made it possible for man to avail himself of grace. For to the reformers man was totally depraved, unable to serve God, unable to help him-

[2] F. M. Powicke, *Reformation England* (London: Oxford University Press, 1941), p. 6.

self by resort to sacraments, to good deeds, even to prayer. Man's very virtues were vices, since they sprang from love of self, however subtly that love might be disguised. Because man was corrupt, he neither did nor could love God. By favor alone could man be freed from the vice to which his human nature doomed him. Grace granted faith. Man must believe not only in God's power and justice, but also in God's willingness to save some; that is, he must believe in God's grace. Through predestined faith, through faith only, some would be saved.

Calvin admitted that this "clear doctrine of Scripture" raised difficult problems for recalcitrant men, but he evaded the problem by urging preachers to be cautious in presenting his doctrine of predestined damnation for some and predestined salvation for others no more worthy.[3]

This is the original Calvinist doctrine. We shall soon see how it was changed and yet remained the same and, to anticipate, how the paradox implicit in this position was transmitted to generation after generation on the American continent, transmuting itself in the process, but leaving the American mind more susceptible to an acceptance of the contradictory than even the general knowledge of the irrationality of man would allow one to anticipate. Here, however, for our purposes it is all-important to bear in mind that when we say *fallen man*, we mean this whole complex we have just explored; we are speaking of man who can do no good and yet must strive to be good.

Controversy in England developed between the followers of the doctrine of Calvin and the Established Church. The English Church, born in compromise, never was doctrinally clear; the Thirty-Nine Articles which set forth its faith

[3] H. D. Foster, *Collected Papers* (privately printed, 1929), p. 34.

could be interpreted to espouse either predestination or free will. But to Englishmen who believed in predestination, such compromise was perilous. Moreover, the ritualism of the Anglican Church threw emphasis on salvation by works, recalling Rome, with its sacraments having in themselves mechanically saving virtues, with its storehouse of merit upon which weaker souls could draw—by making appropriate sacrifice through payment.

The Anglican clergy heard no confessions, to be sure; they assigned no penances; they intoned no prayers for the dead. All who could read English might explore Scripture for themselves (provided that they were males; a law of 1542 forbade any woman to own a Bible in English). Yet the group which came to be labeled Puritan was not satisfied. When Elizabeth ascended to her dead sister's throne, she did restore Protestantism. But she sought to keep Reform within decent bounds. Faith should be lived, not talked about, and Elizabeth ordered her subjects to avoid "all vain and contentious disputations in matters of religion," an order she tried to make good by putting limits on sermonizing.

Elizabeth tried to set bounds to Reform, but she ruled men who felt confident in an expanding world, and even she encountered increasing opposition toward the end of her reign. The Stuarts arrived as the tide ebbed, and their policy brought England no glory.

Her successor was less confident in his power over men's tongues than Elizabeth. Certainly James I had greater taste for sermons, for all that he had long been captive audience to Scots preachers with the acid of Geneva on their tongues. The Puritan party in the English Church petitioned the king to make further reforms in ritual and discipline and to

authorize a new translation of the Bible. James granted the
second request almost immediately and the fruit of that
grant was the foundation of modern English prose, the
King James Bible. Before the king made up his mind about
the first request, he summoned representatives of the pe-
titioners to hold formal debate with his bishops. At that
conference, the Puritan spokesmen allowed themselves to
be trapped: they suggested that points still in dispute be
turned over to a bishop and his presbyters for definitive
decision.

To the son of Mary Stuart, the word "presbyter" was an
offense. For it was the presbyters, ministers and teaching
elders, who had helped make Mary's position in Scotland
untenable and so driven the queen to exile and to death.

Whatever the theological merit of the Puritans' religious
position, their activity in behalf of that position constituted
a threat to the state in the eyes of the Court party. All good
subjects should worship as their king did. To differ defied
the subordination which was necessary for a well-ordered
community. Yet the emotional charge behind the seventeenth-century demand for uniformity in religion makes
one suspect that people were governed by notions far more
primitive than the preservation of political order: open
practice of a disapproved belief would bring the Lord's
anger upon the community in the form of civil strife, if
not of earthquake, plague, failing harvests, or defeat in war.

And indeed civil war was to be the outcome in England.

For their own salvation and the possible salvation of
others, theologians of the Puritan party worked out a vocabulary—they called it a doctrine—which was designated
as the federal or covenant theology. (*Federal* here means

the relations between the parties, *foedera* in Latin, to any treaty or league.)

This covenant theology did not change the essence of Calvinist ideas; it continued to speak of fallen man and the basic inscrutability of God's dealings. But the federal theology talked of this in terms of the law of contract. God had made a covenant with man, promising to choose some, brands from the burning, for salvation. This willingness to contract constituted God's grace.

To talk of predestination thus, in the language of contract, may seem verbiage rather than intellectual change. Still, thought is colored by the language in which it is cast. People who hear their faith expounded in terms of covenants between God and man in respect to salvation and between men and men in respect to the government of church and state—such people may call their God absolute and be convinced that they believe He is so, but insensibly their concepts will change. It is in this sense that Perry Miller says the covenant theology transformed the God of Calvin and the later Puritans from a despot into something resembling a constitutional executive.[4]

This version of Calvinist thought won enough support in England to gain the distrust and opposition of other groups in the Anglican Church. James made two martyrs and some Puritan clergymen were forced out of their pulpits; others felt harried and cramped, but the Puritan party was not effectively suppressed. Puritans were adept at drawing delicate distinctions and so discovering within the institutions they still cherished and hoped to control what no unregenerate eye could see there. A clergyman of Puritan

---

[4] Perry Miller, *The New England Mind* (New York: The Macmillan Co., 1939), p. 377.

opinion could accept ordination from an Anglican bishop
while inwardly refusing to acknowledge that bishop's authority to ordain. Similarly, the Puritan group within a
parish could accept a minister of its own accord and, by
that acceptance, make his assignment by a lay patron into
an act without meaning in the eyes of God.

For the Puritan party was coming to believe that true
churches were assemblies of men who had freely contracted
with each other and with God to keep His faith. And
Puritans were often able to argue that such true churches
could exist, invisible to all but God and His elect, within the
Anglican fabric. But most Puritans were not satisfied with
so tenuous a churchly presence. Since Anglican pastors
might receive their positions from the lay persons whose
possession of particular estates entitled them to make such
appointments, subject to approval of the bishop—which was
not often refused—control of this privilege was traded in.
Groups of Puritan gentlemen raised money to buy the
right to name pastors as that right came into market. Puritan
laymen also raised money to subsidize lecturers—usually
young clergymen who did not have permanent appointments—who assisted the regular minister by delivering
sermons, and who often seduced his parishioners from orthodoxy by their preaching.

In spite of rules and pronouncements about the conduct
of services, ministers of Puritan opinion officiated without
surplices and sometimes even set the communion table un-
railed in the center of the church in order to avoid the
appearance of functioning at an altar.

Both in preaching and practice, therefore, the Puritan
group was still able to work toward its end: not separation
from but control of the Anglican Church. The Puritans

meant to reform and govern that Church; hard though King James might make their way, they did not intend to break with it.

James' son believed in the divinity that doth hedge a king, but Charles I had little gift for keeping up his fences. He was further handicapped by his anti-Calvinist convictions. James had feared the political consequences of Puritan domination of the Church; with most of Puritan doctrine, he had no basic quarrel. Charles felt otherwise. He married a Catholic princess—which even Puritans might recognize as a necessity of international policy. He made Richard Montague one of his personal chaplains—and this was choice, not policy. Montague spoke for what is called the party of moderate reform in the Church. It preferred an elaboration of decorum in worship. It recognized that a true Church existed in Rome, though embedded in corruption. And it seemed immoderate in acknowledgment of the rights of kings.

Charles further threw the weight of royal power into the scales. He chose the Bishop of London, William Laud, as his principal adviser, and Laud was a leader of the anti-Puritan group. Royal patronage, promotion, pay, power, went to enemies of the Puritan position. In 1628 Charles carried his convictions yet further and ordered the Puritans to stop talking: laymen were to accept, not discuss the Thirty-Nine Articles. Churchmen with problems of interpretation were to accept official pronouncements as sufficient answers.

The following year, Charles dissolved Parliament, for Commons not only refused to grant adequate taxes but also voiced its objection to the direction of royal intervention in church government. Charles ruled without Parliament for the next eleven years. They were years of impotence abroad—without grants of taxes, England's king could scarcely afford to take a strong position against France or Spain—and of effort to impose religious uniformity at home. All Englishmen were to worship in the fashion the king and his archbishop called good. Any man who found fault with their pronouncements would suffer.

Restlessness grew out of the impact of new ideas and pressures but those had the greater influence because the economic world was changing. Price levels in England rose by 200 per cent between 1494 and the middle 1600's. We in the twentieth century may not think this an extraordinarily rapid rise, but we tend to accept change as the norm. In a society committed to relatively fixed status, prices which rose both constantly and irregularly were a continuing source of disturbance. A landholder could no longer assume that the income which assured him the position of a gentleman would keep his children in that state. He must increase his gains, therefore, or see his younger sons slip down on the social ladder. As John Winthrop said, a gentleman was hard put to it to "keep sayle with his equals."

Many in the Puritan party felt threatened with the loss of status in the community at the same time that they faced defeat in their struggle for control of the English Church. Winthrop saw the land "weary of its inhabitants" and the "authority of law used to hinder increase of our people." In order to keep down taxes for poor relief, parishes forbade the building of new cottages, thus making it difficult for laborers to marry. (In a period of high infant mortality, pauper bastards' chances of survival were not likely to explode the population of any English village.) Puritan children, moreover, stood in danger of corruption at schools which were inefficient in discipline, distasteful in doctrine, and "insupportable in their charges." Why then, Winthrop asked, "should we stand striving here?" [5]

Those who agreed with Winthrop turned their eyes toward the American continent, where England had made one successful settlement at Jamestown in Virginia. Even earlier, English fishermen had established at least temporary footholds along the coast of Maine and New Hampshire. The English king had made grants both to individuals and to chartered companies which were a special form of corporation (corporations—these included cities, the Church as a whole, the guilds—had been a familiar form of social organization in Europe since the last centuries of the Roman Empire).

It is not necessary to discuss the tangled business history or the confusing territorial claims of the Virginia Company and the Plymouth Company. Both companies held charters which set forth their rights as corporations: to make rules for their own government and to make sub-grants if they chose. Under such a sub-grant, the Pilgrims came to settle in the New World in 1618 and 1620, before the Puritans did. This group of English artisans and yeomen left England for the Netherlands in order to gain freedom to practice their version of the reformed religion, and they left Leyden because they saw no prospect of prospering there unless they gave up their group identity, and because their children were becoming Dutch. In the New World, the men and women who were to become the Pilgrims saw scope for religious liberty and also opportunity to continue as a prosperous and English community.

[5] Robert C. Winthrop, *Life and Letters of John Winthrop* (Boston: Ticknor and Fields, 1864), pp. 309-10.

Thus even the men of the *Mayflower* sought worldly advantage. This was no less important an objective to the more prosperous and far better-educated Puritan group who came to America at the end of the 1620's. Their leaving was more an admission of defeat than the Pilgrims' moves had been, for the Pilgrims were frankly separatist and the Puritans had tried to win at least a place within the English Church. When royal policy made that impossible, they decided to shift the field of combat. Rather than remain in an England where king and bishop were determined to impose their will, Puritans of the eastern counties of England decided to set up for themselves in a land where neither bishop nor king could trouble them.

To make certain that they would not be interfered with, the leaders of the Puritan group decided that all the stock in their new company should be bought by people who intended to emigrate. Control of the stock and possession of the patent, the document setting down the chartered rights of the Massachusetts Bay Company, would thus lie in the hands of those who planned to leave England; the settlers would not be subject to control by absentee owners.[6]

It may be said that coming events thus cast their shadows before; appropriately, the country where the private corporation was to become so characteristic and important a form of private economic organization actually sprang from the manipulation of corporate stocks and charters.

Yet the people who carried through this maneuver were playing for higher stakes than status or possessions. The leaders of the Massachusetts Bay Company wanted to speak the truth they had learned, to live in accordance with that

[6] T. J. Wertenbaker, *Puritan Oligarchy* (New York: Charles Scribner's Sons, 1947), pp. 31-32.

truth themselves, and to make certain that all who entered their community should conform to the practices of that truth. The psychological and psychoanalytic exploration of man's motives has made historians, who are wary, still more wary of taking men's statements at face value. Yet what men say they believe about the universe and their place in it does affect what they do. Conversely, what men do affects both what they believe and what they say they believe. And men suffer when the beliefs they claim to live by stand in conflict with what they do and with the premises which that action is said to represent.

What did the founders say they believed? How did their belief meet the needs of the situation into which they had put themselves? How did the situation operate to change the belief? In the interplay of the problems which these questions present we find the earliest development of the American paradox.

Scholars have long since abandoned the legend that leadership of colonial America was divided between Southern aristocrats and New England zealots, with money-grubbing Dutchmen and Quakers in the lands between. Men in all sections grubbed for money when they thought money was to be had—keeping their hands as clean of labor as possible—and those who gave society its tone inhabited a common universe of discourse.

For seventeenth-century America, that was the world John Calvin had made and William Ames, the great federal theologian, had developed. The leading ministers of New England had studied at Emanuel College at Cambridge, thus validating Elizabeth's prophecy: When she learned Sir Walter Mildmay was founding a college to train learned teachers for the young Anglican Church, the Queen said:

"So, Sir Walter, you have created a Puritan foundation."
Yet much of the Puritan point of view was exceptional only
in its pertinacious concentration on controlling the very
thoughts of its community.

As a party to the struggle over reforming the Anglican
Church, the Puritan group had never denied the authority
of that Church as an institution. As has been pointed out,
the Puritans objected to its manners and its organization;
they opposed its prescriptions for the conduct of church
services and its retention of an ecclesiastical hierarchy. The
Puritans had no objection to the principle of stringent control of church and community by the best men in it.

The best, of course, were the Lord's elect. The doctrine
that a sovereign God justly chooses some to be saved while
He leaves others to bear deserved damnation is a thoroughly
aristocratic doctrine. For one is predestined to salvation as
one is born into nobility; to quote the Duke of Wellington
on the House of Lords: "There is no damned merit about
it." And, obviously, those predestined to salvation should
rule. Consequently, when the Puritan group achieved political power in the land to which it had removed itself, it
did all it could to give the elect control of the community's
religious and political life.

The first New England generations decreed that only
church members might vote or hold office in the Massachusetts Bay Colony (and in its Connecticut offshoots). And
church membership was limited. In order to be accepted
into the church, the prospective member must face questioning by ministers and ruling elders, show that he understood Scripture, be accepted as a person of suitably godly
life, and make solemn profession of religious "experience,"
of inward conviction that God had given him the ability to

accept His grace and to know himself designed for salvation.

This was a portentous undertaking. Some people were too timid to make such assertions in public—especially if they were modest young women. Others might be bold enough in assertion, but unable to convince those who actually governed the congregation.

And church membership alone did not assure influence. All members had a vote, to be sure, but men were expected to follow the lead of their superiors in education, wealth, and standing. The number of church members was further limited by the fact that the minister and elders were not always eager to increase the number of male church members and thus swell the electorate.

For the founders of Massachusetts intended to set up a community permanently ruled by a self-perpetuating body of "saints," protected against the deterioration which the accident of heredity might bring upon an unexamined aristocracy of blood. This did not mean that they believed in democracy. On the contrary, it was held that no conceivable form of government could be worse than a government of the people. John Cotton could not believe that "God ever did ordain democracy as a fit government either for church or commonwealth" and John Winthrop declared that of all forms of government, democracy was "meanest and worse."

Nevertheless, a limited form of democracy did obtain in the Puritan community, for it was held that secular as well as church government must be based on free covenant in order to constitute an authority truly derived from God. But once chosen to make and enforce laws, magistrates were not to be censured by the voters who had put them into power.[7] Yet some three decades earlier, Puritan spokesmen had declared that, although magistrates might not lawfully be resisted, "that which is against the conscience might without disloyalty be refused." [8]

In political practice, as in religious doctrine, the Puritan solution required men to give full allegiance to what seemed like a contradiction. Government required the consent of the governed, for according to Puritan opinion, government was legitimatized by covenant. Yet in Massachusetts, those who had no voice in church and state were held morally bound to obey governors in whose choice they did not participate and laws in whose making they had no voice. So far as the Massachusetts Bay Colony was concerned, its charter was the relevant covenant. Those who came to live there were considered to have given their consent to the government which its charter had created. And since that government was designed to be controlled by the few, their consent bound all.

John Cotton was more obviously inconsistent when he wrote: "It is necessary that all power be limited, Church power or other, . . ." [9] Yet he helped draft the Cambridge Platform of 1648, and according to that, the church might call upon the state to punish not only blasphemy and idolatry but also "venting corrupt and pernicious opinions . . . ," surely an unbridled extension of church power.

The state did punish those opinions. It barred "foreign" proponents of outrageous doctrine. When people like the Quakers persisted in coming to Massachusetts, the Puritan state discouraged them with whip and gallows. Even more

---

[7] Perry Miller, *Orthodoxy in Massachusetts* (Cambridge: Harvard University Press, 1933), p. 228.

[8] Ibid., p. 33.

[9] Ibid., p. 226.

earnestly, perhaps, the community sought to preserve the purity of the Puritan solution against assaults from within.

Such assaults might come from resistance by unregenerate residents, from the enthusiasm of the regenerate, or from the effective assertion of independence by congregations. The resistance of the unregenerate was easiest to handle. Since many of the rejected accepted the premises upon which they were excluded, they constituted only a minor threat to the ruling group. Neither the rejected nor those who never presented themselves as candidates for church membership resisted being taxed to support the church; they rarely protested being fined five shillings (no small sum in the early seventeenth century) for each absence from meeting. For most New Englanders agreed that a man might be compelled to listen to sermons that might touch his heart and bring him out of brutishness if not into salvation.

The Puritan solution was more threatened by the redeemed. And none of the redeemed was more troublesome than the Reverend John Wheelwright and Mrs. Anne Hutchinson. In Boston, Mrs. Hutchinson and her friends met to recapitulate the latest sermon, which was considered a peculiarly appropriate way to use leisure hours. Too often, however, sober summary turned into discussion. Mrs. Hutchinson and her friends were said to assert that only two ministers, the renowned John Cotton and the less eminent John Wheelwright, were truly preaching a covenant of grace; the others all labored under a covenant of works. Mrs. Hutchinson and her followers frequently left the meetinghouse when others preached or, when the sermon was over, they asked troublesome questions (putting questions for enlightenment was still often part of religious exercises).

Such arguing,[10] and by women at that, struck at the roots of good order, and the danger was the greater because of the doctrine which animated the questioning, though that doctrine was in large part closer to the original Calvinist doctrine from which, Mrs. Hutchinson claimed, many ministers were moving away. (As a matter of fact, they were, but this they would not admit.)

She and her partisans—they were not all women, incidentally, and Mrs. Hutchinson would probably have insisted that the doctrine was Cotton's, Calvin's, and God's, and in no way her own—held that nothing external, such as behavior, constituted evidence of salvation. Only the Christian himself could know whether he were saved, and that knowledge belonged to him and God alone. Further, in the regenerate there was no sin to repent of. (It is this that contradicts accepted Calvinist doctrine.)

The rulers of Massachusetts called the Hutchinson group *antinomians*, anarchists in our terms. But they in turn called their rulers *formalists* and, with asperity, empty husks of doctrine. Controversy raged in pulpit and at the fireside. The Reverend John Wheelwright, on whose support Anne Hutchinson relied, insisted that however holy people might seem in their actions, if they trusted to external evidence of their righteousness they stood in danger of spiritual death.[11] Those who opposed Wheelwright and Mrs. Hutchinson held that external signs, that is, behavior, constituted reasonably valid evidence of salvation. Exclusive dependence on inner certainty would necessarily beguile the weak—and on this level all men were weak—into contempt for law, for the

---

[10] Charles Francis Adams, *Three Episodes of Massachusetts History* (Boston: Houghton Mifflin, 1892), p. 401.
[11] Ibid., pp. 402-404.

external constraints which were needed to hold the natural man in check since even in the regenerate the natural man still lived.

Authority, civil and spiritual, acted. In 1673 church and magistrates assembled to deal with the problem and to settle the community's mind, first moving the seat of their deliberations from pro-Hutchinson Boston to the more amenable community of Newton, as Cambridge was then called. The settlement was achieved, so far as doctrine was concerned, by drawing up a list of heresies, among them the antinomian notion that the regenerate were no longer sinful. Maintenance of heresy was punished by fine (20 shillings a month for the first six months; 40 shillings a month for the next half year) or banishment. Mrs. Hutchinson was tried for sedition and contempt, and banished, as everyone knows. John Wheelwright had been banished a few months earlier for the same offenses, and he took himself and his opinions to New Hampshire. Of the 74 persons whom the colony proceeded against, 41 either acknowledged their errors or merely stopped talking; 33 left for other settlements. The Reverend Mr. Cotton bowed to the judgment of his fellow ministers so far as the banishments were concerned, but ". . . it was thought he did still retain his own sense and enjoy his own apprehension in all or most of the things then controverted. . . ." [12]

Authority thus had its way with the disruptive factor of emotionalism in Puritan piety. It was also to have its way with what it considered excessive independence among the congregations.

As Puritan thought developed in England, John Cotton

[12] Brooks Adams, *Emancipation of Massachusetts: The Dream and the Reality* (Boston: Houghton Mifflin, 1919), p. 231.

had made himself spokesman for the belief that each congregation should govern itself. For the congregation was the true church, the body of believers gathered in the Lord's name, covenanting with Him and each other to worship purely and choosing the minister who was to serve, teach, and lead them toward that goal. To preserve unity, however, the congregations of the Bay Colony gathered in synods to take counsel together and to admonish those who stood in error. And the synod commanded the aid of the civil authorities. An obstinate congregation might attempt to disregard counsel and admonition, but its willfulness would not go unpunished. Even William Ames—the eminent Cambridge theologian who had been deprived of his post in Christ Church College for refusing to wear the surplice—agreed that civil government might act to root out "false ministers and counterfeit worship." [13]

Again, when Salem tried to keep Roger Williams as its minister, it had to fight both synod and legislature. Williams contradicted the body of Puritan opinion which held, with Cotton, that New Englanders need not formally separate themselves from the Church of England. Roger Williams would not, he said, minister to an "unseparated people." [14] In order to have him as its pastor, the Salem church made the declaration of disaffiliation that Williams desired, and he accepted their call. He was not installed, however, for that required the agreement of the magistrates, and Williams had aroused their antagonism by attacking the supervisory function of the customary joint meetings of the clergy. These meetings, he declared, destroyed the spiritual liberty of the congregation. Nevertheless, in 1634, after

[13] T. J. Wertenbaker, *op. cit.*, p. 74.
[14] Ibid., p. 25.

two years of wrangling, Salem won its fight; Williams' ministry was officially acknowledged. But he continued to be "stiff-necked," attacking oaths of loyalty which required all Massachusetts residents to submit to the ruling group, and also preaching in defense of the Indians' right to their land. The following year, Williams was banished because he had spread "new and dangerous opinions against authority of magistrates." [15]

That winter, Williams and a few followers moved away from the settlements into the Rhode Island wilderness. Such a move was not easy—breaking a dwelling place out of the forest demanded bitter effort—but it was possible. In the possibility of moving off onto property of one's own lay the threat to excessively rigorous action to maintain any kind of control over the colonists. Williams did have a difficult struggle to keep the Rhode Island settlements out of the grasp of Massachusetts Bay, but he was able to do so, partly because the Stuarts were restored in 1660, and the Bay Colony could not thereafter safely impose its will by force.

In 1663, Williams secured a royal charter for Rhode Island and Providence Plantation, thus assuring the autonomy of those settlements. Meanwhile, the Bay Colony was compelled to permit public worship according to the Book of Common Prayer. Later, it was also required to make ownership of property sufficient qualification for voting. Finally, in 1691, after nearly ten years of litigation, of diplomatic negotiations by representatives of the colony, and even of abortive efforts by James II to set up a new and absolutist regime in New England, the Massachusetts Bay Company was forced to give up its old corporate charter and the

[15] Ibid., pp. 305-306.

colony accepted a new one. This charter imposed further restrictions, requiring the colony, among other things, to accept a governor appointed by the king.

Some of the changes were more in form than in fact, to be sure. Property holders demanding the vote had to produce certificates of good character, if they were not church members, and the minister and the local congregation, as well as the town selectmen, had power to deny those certificates.

Actually, English pressure was less effective in modifying Puritan rigidity than was the growth of the community in the frontier context. Settlements multiplied and, as people moved inland, it became even more difficult for any central authority effectively to supervise their behavior. The economy developed as settlements spread out, and that development brought New Englanders into the orbit of a larger economic world than subsistence agriculture or even raising export staples such as tobacco could have provided. New England's economic life was soon involved with commerce, with shipbuilding—New Englanders even sold their vessels in England—with trading in fish and lumber and furs. As population rose and wealth grew, men moved out of the groups into which they had beeen born, and the likelihood that, with an expanding economic life, the movement would be upward was of prime significance.

For centuries, most men had lived and expected to live according to the patterns of behavior common in the groups in which their forebears had lived. Not only economics but the very conditions of life in a new country softened the edges of inherited patterns, weakening them as psychological supports, but also lessening the constrictions which they imposed. Because movement, physical and social, was more

possible in New England than in the older country, and
particularly because property was easier to acquire, social
change became the rule rather than the regrettable exception.

But change has always awakened countercurrents. Change
was not accepted by the pious; rather it was taken to mean
backsliding, falling away from the ideals of the fathers and
worshipping idols willfully chosen. In 1673 Thomas Shepard, one of the most noteworthy of the early Puritan
pastors, warned his congregation of what he considered
signs of impending degeneracy; some people did not understand that it was "Satan's policy to plead for an indefinite
and boundless toleration," [16] to seek to confine the "sword
of the civil magistrate to its scabbard," [17] and to forget how
"woeful would the state of things soon be among us if men
might have the liberty without control to profess or preach
or print or publish what they list tending to the Seduction
of others. . . ." [18] Within the congregations, furthermore,
Shepard said there reigned a spirit of "sovereign unsociable
rigid independence" [19] in contrast to the time when "if help
[from the synod] were not asked it was sent them without
asking" and none formerly called that "an infringement of
church liberty." [20] Contempt for authority was growing;
elementary schools were in decay; many families neither
prayed nor owned a whole Bible. Children were fractious,
parents indulgent, sons "so proud and stubborn" that they

---

[16] Thomas Shepard, *Eye-Salve or a Watch-Word from our Lord
. . . to Take Heed of Apostacy . . .*, Election Sermon, *May 15, 1672*
(Boston, 1673. Microfilm, Columbia University), p. 14.
[17] Ibid., p. 21.
[18] Ibid., p. 38.
[19] Ibid., p. 23.
[20] Ibid., p. 29.

would not work for their fathers without wages.[21] Magistrates needed the help of the ministers and the Lord in order to "crush profaneness, pride and Drunkenness and whoredome and Lying and Stealing, the Heresies and Schismes and factions and such works of the Flesh and scandalous disorders that do so lamentably prevail among us. . . ." [22]

Ten years later, Urian Oakes, minister and President of Harvard, saw New England gone from bad to worse. Hypocrites had grown "saucy" in spirit and railed at the Lord for not rewarding their prayers. Worship was declining in fervor: How "cold dead and sleepy" were prayers in families; how "dull and drowzie [was the] work of days of humiliation." [23] People neglected the Lord until some "terrible Sermon or some dangerous sickness" roused them to prayer and reformation. Then they relapsed and were "as bad as ever." [24] New Englanders wanted "smooth things, not right things." [25] Those who called themselves religious could "tipple it, and swill it, and keep vain company and spend their time in idle chat" and deride the "precision" of better men.[26]

Earnest preachers, clergymen or lay, have generally tended to deplore the decline of manners and morality in their time. But New Englanders like Oakes and Shepard were recognizing reality; their world was indeed moving beyond the kind of domination which the leaders of the founding Puritan generation had been able to exert. Some

[21] Ibid., pp. 22, 50.
[22] Ibid., p. 41.
[23] Urian Oakes, *Seasonable Discourse* (Cambridge, Massachusetts, 1682, Fast Sermon. Microfilm, Columbia University), p. 7.
[24] Ibid., p. 10.
[25] Ibid., p. 18.
[26] Ibid., p. 30.

of the changes were of external origin, as has been shown, but those were no more significant than the alterations which had occurred and were occurring in the Puritan churches themselves. Those changes reflected the new currents of thought and feeling which rose during the eighteenth century. In the next chapter, therefore, we shall be concerned with the hardening of Puritan attitudes, and with the great upsurge which broke through the dry "cake" of Puritan custom.

New World Necessities 3

WHEN JOHN COTTON insisted that members of the New England churches need not formally renounce the Church of England, he expressed a significant fact about the people who founded the mainland colonies: they had left England, but they did not intend to abandon England's civilization. The ruling group among the settlers had long proclaimed their purpose to be separation from abuses, not separation from the tradition which those abuses deformed. Few colonists moved into the wilderness in order to lapse into a comfortable barbarism although, once men had familiarized themselves with the grain that grew in the new country and learned how to hunt there, such a lapse would have been relatively easy. A small population could certainly have enjoyed a shiftless plenty. Fur, fish, and lumber would have paid for iron and salt, and a regressive community would have needed little else from outside.

But the mainland colonists intended to continue to be a part, however provincial, of the world they had left. They struggled to stay alive within the economic and intellectual frame of reference which they had brought with them. Since that frame of reference was irrelevant in many instances, those striving to maintain it became increasingly alienated, as will appear more clearly when we turn to the

nineteenth century, with its tug and countertug between
democracy and oligarchy, between the commands of gen-
tility and the pursuit of unlimited wealth, between the desire for social stability and an unrestrained economic growth
whose social consequences could not be calculated.

From the later seventeenth century onward, efforts to
maintain the traditional framework generated desires, which
could not be easily satisfied, for a cultivated society. These
ultimately created one of the characteristic figures in the
American landscape of loneliness—the person who had developed cultivated tastes but was sentenced to live in the
bog of crass materialism which was the American small
town.

The mainland colonists had, then, to do more than keep
themselves alive, to increase and multiply in the wilderness.
They had to make that wilderness yield something which
the older society would buy in order that the colonists
might pay for the things which would keep the values of
that older society in being among them. From the fish-
drying platforms of the New Hampshire coast to the low-
lands of Carolina, the colonists therefore stood committed
to the European economy. And in their commitment lay
the seed of a varied economic development.

Had the colonies possessed mines of precious metals, had
they all produced acceptable agricultural staples, such as
tobacco, had their source of furs been unlimited, then the
mainland colonies might have easily fitted into the pattern
of trade accepted as proper to their dependent status in
relation to the mother country, that is, primarily as sup-
pliers of the raw materials necessary for her consumption,
manufacture, or trade. They would have developed, but
their development would have produced a relatively simple

economy. In the absence of these commodities either in sufficient quantity or of the desired kind, some of the mainland colonies had to diversify their economic life. Iron-masters soon were working the ore-bearing sands of New Jersey because England not only allowed pig iron to be imported but even encouraged its production. Later, they exploited the forests for charcoal with which to smelt the more rewarding iron deposits in Virginia and Pennsylvania. In other areas, colonists became ingenious middlemen, merchant-shipowners who carried plantation products overseas, who exchanged fish and lumber produced by their fellow mainlanders for West Indian molasses, in the famous triangular trade, who owned shares in distilleries which converted that molasses into rum, who used that rum as a medium of exchange with which slaves were procured to maintain the production of sugar in the Caribbean and to keep the output of tobacco expanding on the mainland.

In this fashion the mainland colonies developed, during the late seventeenth and early eighteenth century, an economy which was not entirely dependent upon the production of agricultural staples for export, although those staples did continue to be the most important items in colonial foreign commerce. Nevertheless, ingenuity could rarely produce a favorable balance of trade for the mainland colonies—as a rule, what they bought was more expensive than what they sold. Still, their businessmen learned to cope with the shifts of a complicated economy rather better than did the Southern planters who so often found themselves debtors in British factors' hands. And, as our contemporary economic historians point out, the habits of managing and the talents of the entrepreneur are exceedingly important in helping communities change from simple traditional economies to more complex modern societies.

The amenities proper to a complicated, civilized economic way of life cost far more, proportionately, than they did in Europe. Time after time, from the seventeenth-century immigrant who had no possessions but his power to work to the twentieth-century refugee professional or artist, we hear that America is a fine country for laborers but a difficult place for people accustomed to ease and deference. The colonies, and later the young and the maturing United States, were described, time after time, as no place for people with some small income and a taste for books and cultivated company.

Such tastes were considered proper, even in the seventeenth century; they were considered to be part of the world with which the colonists tried to maintain their ties. Yet the very struggle to achieve the material base for indulging those tastes tended to inhibit their development. The economic growth which alone could produce the necessary surplus demanded a single-minded pursuit of money, and the man who was effectively single-minded in that pursuit had little energy for anything else. Often, therefore, the effort to live in accordance with some of the values of the older culture tended to isolate the individual and make him feel lonely. The struggle to stay alive and to be economically productive generated the sort of person who had no true link to the older world to which the unhappy few continued to owe allegiance and to which education and the church long continued to give lip service. Thus, as accumulation proceeded and the material base needed for existence on a more cultivated level grew broader, taste for existence on that level did not keep pace with the growth of population or wealth. Finally, in the nineteenth century, we see dedication to the unbridled accumulation of money become the one truly masculine pattern of life. Making money was socially acceptable. Practicing a profession was tolerable, if it were lucrative enough, but the disinterested love of learning did not seem truly manly; artistic creativity was generally suspect, and enjoying the arts was a woman's pastime.

Throughout its history "plain living and high thinking" has had relatively few exponents in the United States. Today, maintaining congenial circles of cultivated persons is difficult if not impossible in small towns and some of the larger cities. Amenities of that sort may actually have been rather more attainable in some of the closely settled villages of the mid-seventeenth century than they were to become later. Thomas Jefferson did not design Montpelier for Madison and Ashlawn for Monroe merely to show off his gifts as an amateur architect. Jefferson wanted conversable people within riding distance.

Good society might be essentially an amenity, an adornment which men subject to the necessities of life in a new country might be obliged to forgo or certainly postpone indefinitely. Education stood in a rather different position. Certainly, education was essential for a cultivated life. But it had a more fundamental function. Education was necessary if the mainland colonists were to carry out their purpose and keep within the orbit of the most valued aspects of the culture they had left behind. Without basic literacy, Christian laymen would be shut away from the source of their faith: to the man who could not read, Scripture in the vernacular was not a real presence. Without the essentials of classical learning, the Puritans held, pastors could not be properly trained and Christian laymen would be left to the ministry of ignorant enthusiasts.

In the Northern Colonies at least, gestures were made toward public support of both objectives: a literate laity and a learned ministry. In many instances, gestures remained only gestures; although law required towns to maintain elementary schools, no one saw to it that the law was effectively enforced. Colleges were established in Harvard's wake, but they offered a mediocre level of instruction. Yet the struggle continued; if formal education declined in quality, the Puritan sermon kept alive the desire to be logical in contention. Only a few men wrote poetry in the colonies; the novel was still an undeveloped literary form; and colonial towns had little place for the drama although, in 1735, Charleston did have a theater. Thereafter, the colonies offered an audience for plays, but they did not support any local dramatists. Intellectual life still justified itself in terms of utility, not delight. Men might divert themselves with the study of natural philosophy and natural history, to be sure; they might discover plants, observe the planets, describe diseases, and even try to introduce new methods for coping with them. Cotton Mather supported inoculation (not vaccination, of course), the direct infection with smallpox in hope of a mild attack and subsequent immunity—a hope surprisingly often justified. Mather's older contemporary, John Winthrop, Jr., who was elected a member of the Royal Society in 1663, predicted the discovery of a fifth satellite to Jupiter, a prediction which could not be verified until astronomical instruments had been improved sufficiently to check Winthrop's calculations. Winthrop's great-grandnephew, another John Winthrop, set up the first laboratory in experimental physics in

America. Later, he directed the first colonial scientific expedition. This went to Newfoundland in 1761 in order to study the transit of Venus. Under his guidance, Americans, for the first time, participated in an international project to increase man's knowledge.

Such scientific interests were considered a sort of recreation, however; the intellectual had more serious concerns: the ancient languages, theology, and philosophy. For these were the means by which men might be influenced to maintain and develop a particular kind of life. The struggle to maintain the higher learning, at least, may be regarded as part of the effort to retain control of colonial life in the hands of its founders. We have seen the ways in which the leaders of the Puritan colonies attempted to keep secular power in the hands of the elect. In Chapter 2 we have seen the intrusion of English jurisdiction upon the political structure of that effort. That intrusion did not modify the oligarchical character of that structure; nor did it change the religious justification for the domination of a few wiser and better men (though none was wise nor good) over the body of those who were worse.

Religious fervor had been diminishing for a generation, as was shown by the number of respectable persons who could not sincerely claim to have experienced assurance that they were saved. By 1662 the Half-way Covenant recognized this situation, permitting those who led exemplary lives, although they were not church members, to have their children baptized. Baptism would not of itself save an infant's soul, to be sure, but it did show that he was a member of the Christian community, a person whose parents had care for his spiritual future. When grown, such people had no voice in church affairs nor might they receive communion, unless they became church members, as not too many of them did. Nevertheless, as they married these young people, who had been baptized on sufferance, presented their own children for baptism.

At this point, many earnest men began to be concerned about the tenuous bond between the church and these sons of the Half-way Covenant. Congregations in which such persons were numerous could scarcely maintain the old level of Puritan piety.

That piety had always been marked by decorum. As Perry Miller points out, the Puritans sought for "a plain style" in their religious life as in their sermons; they wanted neither displays of rhetoric nor the whipping up of emotion. Sober argument, somberly presented—this was the staple of discourse from the pulpit, twice each Sunday and usually once more during the week.

Sobriety in a context of peril may be dramatic, and the wilderness provided peril in abundance—the harshness of making a living, the threat of epidemic disease, the danger of attack by the Indians, the exertions of the devil. All these, New England had experienced and recorded by the beginning of the eighteenth century, but New England was not alone in such experience, although it was most zealous in its recording. Chopping a farm out of the forest was as hard work in Maryland, Virginia, or the Carolinas as it was in New England, and there were few slaves before the middle seventeenth century. Malaria and smallpox spared no area of the colonies. The Pequots were not the only Indians to attack, although their onslaughts against New England were particularly well organized. The devil had his votaries in New York and Virginia as well as in Massachusetts, although fewer people were legally accused as witches, and none of those charged outside New England is recorded as being executed.

As settlements grew older in colony after colony, visible perils receded, and as they diminished, the devil seemed to lose power to afflict men through such human servants as witches. But though few were willing to make formal covenants to obey him, the devil exerted his influence in subtler and more dangerous ways. Joshua Scottow, a Puritan minister of the younger generation, had expressed his fear lest the New England church be no longer Solomon's garden enclosed but only a meadow fenced in, a "receptacle of standing waters," of "formal nominal Christians destitute of the life and power of godliness." Boston was become a "lost town" where women "affect strange and fantastic fashions, naked backs and bare Breasts." No man now "mourned on the mountains his own iniquities," none broke down the wall of his "Adamantine heart." [1]

What, Scottow asked, is become of "the primitive Zeal, Piety, and Holy Heat?" and he answered, "The soul's lively Thirsting after God and His ways" had been "metamorphosed into Land and Trade . . . renewing of the mind into conformity with the present evil world. . . . Religion hath brought forth Riches, but the Daughter hath devoured the mother as was said and observed of old." [2]

Scottow spoke in 1691, but the trend he deplored continued. The New England churches, those of Massachusetts and Connecticut particularly, maintained their original doctrine: only the converted were fit to become members of

[1] Joshua Scottow, *Old Men's Tears for their own Declensions Mixed with Tears of their . . . Fears of their . . . Further Falling off from New-England's Primitive Constitution* . . . (Boston ?, 1691. Microfilm, Columbia University), p. 6.

[2] Ibid., p. 11.

the body of Christ which was the visible church. Yet to many, even in Puritan New England, it no longer seemed appropriate to label numbers of worthy persons religiously worthless. Nor did it seem likely that people who were prosperous and well behaved would allow themselves to be kept in a position of second-class citizenship indefinitely.

Some Bostonians, at least, settled the problem by remodeling their church organization. The Brattle Street congregation set up on its own in 1698. It not only used the Lord's Prayer and read the Bible without comment, thus approaching Anglican forms of worship; it even gave noncommunicants a voice in church government. It went further, admitting persons to full church membership without requiring them to make a public confession: to state that they had repented the sin of their existence and that they had experienced grace and so felt themselves to be saved. By waiving this requirement, the Brattle Streeters gave up the Puritan concept of the church as a covenanted assembly of the saved.

The Reverend Nicholas Noyes of Salem wrote the venturesome congregation a "letter of admonition and rebuke," but the elders paid him no mind.[3] Noyes had been minister of the church at Salem during the witch trials of 1692; he would scarcely be taken for authority by a congregation which had Thomas Brattle among its lay leaders, for Brattle had expressed his opposition to the Salem witch hunt—in a letter discreetly circulated among his friends.

Acceptance of the Brattle Street congregation by the other Boston churches legitimatized what seemed like a return to formalism. The growth of the Anglican Church in Boston, slow though it was, showed that ceremonial, too,

[3] T. J. Wertenbaker, *Puritan Oligarchy*, p. 147.

was becoming acceptable even to some whose grandfathers had left England rather than worship according to the forms of the Anglican liturgy. Whether in Brattle Street or King's Chapel, the new current seemed to justify the foreboding of preachers like Scottow and Urian Oakes. The churches themselves, according to such opinion, were confounding God and Mammon, taking prosperous and decent lives for evidence that souls were saved.

But throughout history, many men have asked that their faith give them more than just a sanction for accepting the social order. Traditionally, religion has been one of the approved channels through which men and women encounter the kind of heightened experience which we call ecstasy. The Puritans, as has been said, were intellectual in their faith and, in their worship, they avoided not only ritual but also claimed to avoid "enthusiasm," which was no term of praise in the seventeenth century but rather a label for what we should call unbridled emotionalism. Nevertheless, along with the strictness of their theology, the early Puritans did achieve an ecstasy which we may find difficult to differentiate from the enthusiasm they condemned. Certainly, they sought ecstasy. Sometimes it welled up out of solitary meditation; sometimes it came during a particularly moving sermon; sometimes the experience came to many people at once. Then whole congregations might feel a new serenity, living in a "season of sweetness," to use the contemporary phrase.

When long periods passed and such experiences did not recur, people felt anxious. They accused themselves of hardness of heart and feared that they would never receive grace. Yet some people distrusted their own emotional responsiveness even while they longed to be roused.

And in the early 1730's, their longings began to be answered, as the movement known as the Great Awakening rose and spread through the colonies, leaving a permanent mark on American religious behavior. In its varied aspects, the Awakening illustrates the tension between passivity and earnest seeking in religion and the interplay between that tension and the experiences of loneliness and anxiety. It further illustrates the currents of anxiety which its intense evangelism roused, allayed, and roused again as it led men to a conviction of redemption through a conviction of sin.

As we shall see, the Awakening appeared first on the frontier, and the particular needs of frontier life colored it to a remarkable degree. The first Puritan generation had been a frontier people, physically isolated, standing alone with a wrathful God whom they had come to the wilderness to serve. Always zealous, their need for God was in no way diminished by the hardships of the New World. To them, religion was both a source of anxiety and its most effective cure. As the older settlements prospered, the isolation of the settlers diminished and the church was no longer the only focus of sociability, the one place where people met for some broader purpose than carrying on the business of daily life.

In the newer settlements, however, men continued to relive some of the experience of the founders. Never again, to be sure, would Europeans settle where none of their kind had stood. Later settlers were usually preceded by explorers, trappers, hunters, or even surveyors and scouts for land speculators. Yet continuously after 1650, people moved farther into wild country. Within three generations after the first planting of the mainland colonies, the pattern of American settlement was set: the older communities would begin to resemble English provincial towns or cities —safe and stable, with wolves and Indians dangers less likely to be met with than were highwaymen on the unpoliced English roads. But while the older settlements were becoming more European, some of their people moved on —not far in terms of measured distance perhaps, but far enough to require a different way of life.

Once a man passed beyond the outlying farms and crude roadways of pre-railroad America, he stood in unbroken forest or stubborn-soiled prairie, alone with his family, when he had a family, cut off from the world he had left, supported only by his own determination to meet the needs of his existence. Then, as more families moved into the area, the struggle to live became somewhat less bitter. Men could exchange work and goods. They could give each other psychological sustenance, too. And aside from sheer human companionship, that sustenance came mainly from religion and education, for religion provided a measure of emotional support, and education, in the shape of basic literacy, made the Bible accessible to the men who pressed inland from the seaboard.

Generation after generation, from the 1640's on, such experiences were repeated. Generation after generation, some Americans lived on the fringe of settlements while others to the east were becoming more sophisticated. Generation after generation, the church and religion continued to be the moving frontier's principal bulwark against loneliness and, accordingly, people who lived on the frontier experienced the psychological impact of the contradiction between the faith which said man is a creature without power to act to save his soul and the demands of an environment which made intense effort the condition of his existence. Nevertheless, religion was not the primary motive which took the pioneer into the wilderness, and his fervor tended to be unstable. Religious excitement could rise and run high in forest darkness where cold, wolves, Indians—present and anticipated—sharpened fear and intensified the need for solace, but frequently excitement ebbed as swiftly as it rose. God returned from men's hearts to His heavenly throne, and the temperature of religious concern moderated.

The history of Northampton, then on the border of settlement in Massachusetts, illustrates several phases of the swell and slackening of piety. For more than five decades, Solomon Stoddard served the town as its pastor. Although he may not have wholly agreed with the rather worldly Bostonians who organized the Brattle Street congregation, Stoddard introduced practices which were not too unlike theirs. After 1704 he admitted people who had not had experience of grace to the communion table and he persuaded neighboring congregations to do likewise. For Stoddard regarded the sacrament as a means of achieving grace.[4] But Stoddard also accepted God's absolute power and the certain damnation of those He did not choose to save.

Since Stoddard was both a strict moralist and warmly pious, he felt that he had reason to deplore the frivolity of the sheep whose shepherd he was. His preaching would waken the congregation to a sense of its spiritual peril. People suffered in their awareness; they repented, and some came forward to testify that they knew themselves to be saved. Then fervor would dwindle. Conversions came less frequently. The town lapsed into careless ways: finery

[4] Jonathan Edwards, *Works of President Edwards,* Vol. I (New York: S. P. Converse, 1829), pp. 110, 301.

flaunted on Sunday; husking bees, with every young man
who found a red ear entitled to kiss the girl of his choice;
and, it was rumored, dancing.

As Stoddard aged, his congregation called an assistant
minister, his grandson, Jonathan Edwards. The younger
man succeeded Stoddard as pastor in 1723, but Northampton was unresponsive to his astringent eloquence. Then suddenly, in 1733, a young slut announced herself convinced,
first of her sinfulness, and then of her firm belief that God
had forgiven her. Soon afterward, for no known reason, a
young man died and then a young matron. The three events
seem to have been crucial. The hamlet where the two young
people had lived, and died so unexpectedly, was dismayed
and roused to a new concern for religion.[5] The whole
Northampton congregation caught fire; converts ranged in
age from ninety to precocious four.

News of the Lord's work spread from Northampton.
Soon all the thinly settled Connecticut Valley was afire.
In Edwards' phrase, God rode "forth in the chariot of His
salvation, conquering and to conquer." The frontier had
rediscovered religion.[6]

The Great Awakening affected all the colonies. The
1740's incidentally were characterized by an upsurge of
religious concern all through Protestant Europe. For a long
time, historians attributed the Great Awakening of 1741-
43 in the colonies to the preaching of a celebrated English
evangelist, George Whitefield, who came to America in
1740 and, from Georgia to Massachusetts, roused men's
souls, even charming the silver out of Benjamin Franklin's

[5] Ibid., I, 121.
[6] Edwin S. Gaustad, *The Great Awakening in New England* (New
York: Harper, 1957), p. 19.

pocket. Recent research has shown how the ground was prepared for Whitefield by the Presbyterians of the Middle Colonies—especially in backwoods New Jersey—and by pastors like Edwards himself. For these men were invited to preach to many congregations and their message traveled far from their remote homes.

Those who supported the Awakening soon found themselves caught in multiple tensions. Here, Jonathan Edwards may serve as an example. Edwards is best remembered as the preacher of God's wrath, but he also preached His abounding love. His sermons made people weep and swoon and sing noisily. Edwards was convinced that only such stirring of the emotions could bring the natural man into a state where God's love and grace could penetrate the spirit. Yet after fifteen years and a variety of disillusioning experiences, Edwards wondered whether rousing men to religious turmoil did not injure their spiritual life. He feared that the experience of religious emotion might become an end in itself; men would no longer care for truth and goodness; they would not be concerned with the logical basis of their beliefs or even the character of their lives.

Thus, ironically, Edwards, who had been so important in the revival of religion, reached a position very like that of some of the people who had opposed the Awakening from its first appearance. The new movement, they had said, threatened both authority and decency. Its preaching was too forthright, too pungent and direct. Its impact upon women was dangerous, for it encouraged them to pay more attention to the pleasure of hearing an evangelist preach than to their household duties. Anglican rector Timothy Cutler said that since the Awakening began, Boston's presses were "forever teeming with books and our women with

bastards." A contemporary Congregationalist minister de-
nounced the Awakening for engendering enthusiasm which
tried to "destroy all property, to make all things common,
wives as well as goods." [7] Other preachers attacked the
movement on more strictly theological grounds; its pre-
sumption to know how grace could be attained constituted
original sin, one minister said.[8]

Such public disputes among ministers stimulated con-
tentiousness among laymen. Here the example of Northampton is again instructive. Although Jonathan Edwards
had a notable European reputation as theologian and philos-
opher, his flock finally rejected his guidance in respect to
both conduct and theology. A petty dispute over Edwards'
attempt to keep local young people free of contamination
by books he called "lascivious" roused anger and prolonged
wrangling. At about the same time, Edwards began to insist that some who had claimed saving religious experience
two years earlier, during the revival of 1742, had fallen into
spiritual pride because of that conviction. This must have
seemed increasingly puzzling to many Northampton people
as they witnessed what they must have thought of as his
own spiritual pride. For during the next five years, Edwards
gradually became convinced that the theological position
which had been held by his grandfather, Solomon Stoddard, by the Northampton congregation, and even by himself, was actually a dangerous error.

As has been mentioned, Stoddard believed that, like love
in an arranged marriage, saving faith was most likely to
come after entry into the church and partaking of com-

[7] Ibid., pp. 31, 32.
[8] Ibid., p. 78.

munion. In 1749 Jonathan Edwards told his congregation
that he had returned to the earlier Puritan position and no
longer believed, as they did, that knowledge of Scripture
and a blameless life were sufficient for church membership.
Those who sought the privileges of members, he now believed, should make a profession of sanctifying grace in
some way that would satisfy the minister; however, the
applicant need not make the profession publicly. Edwards
urged that he and his congregation reason together over his
change of opinion, but the Northampton congregation refused. Pastor and flock then fell into another acrimonious
wrangle which ended with the most eminent theologian
New England had produced being dismissed by a provincial
church because he had rejected the temper of the time.

Edwards might have drawn some members of his congregation to his own view, but he considered setting up a
new church as contrary to his duty. Other ministers were
less scrupulous about avoiding divisive action. The heart-
searching and contentions roused by the Awakening
prompted separation in many congregations. The revivals
also brought new support to denominations which had not
yet become generally important. Before we consider the
various sects, it may be wise to refresh our memory as to
their differing beliefs and organization. We are here concerned, in varying degree, with four different sects: the
Congregationalists (the descendants of the Puritans), the
Presbyterians, the Baptists, and the Methodists (these last,
however, did not become a major factor in the American
religious scene until after the Revolution). Congregationalists, Presbyterians, and Baptists alike by and large accepted
the Calvinist creed; the Baptists differed from the other two

in that they rejected infant baptism. Congregationalists and Baptists were organized as independent churches. The Presbyterians had a representative form of church government by synods of ministers and assemblies in which both laymen and ministers participated. The Methodists,[9] an offshoot of the Church of England, believed in free will and were differentiated from the parent church by their evangelistic enthusiasm; their church government was episcopal.

Now, to return to the consequences of the Great Awakening. The Presbyterians won most new members as a result of that movement and it was among Presbyterians that the religious upheaval of 1741-42 produced some of its most divisive results.

The Philadelphia Synod, which finally split apart as a result of dissension provoked by the Awakening, was the most important Presbyterian body in the Middle Colonies, where the denomination was strongest. In large measure, the dissensions stemmed from the work of William Tennent and his son Gilbert and the group of young ministers who followed their example. Gilbert Tennent by his preaching and his father by his work as an educator had helped create the evangelical climate in which revivalism flourished even before 1733 when the ferment began in Jonathan Edwards' congregation.

Gilbert Tennent's preaching attacked spiritual complacency; it insisted that mere profession of correct belief and maintenance of seemly behavior did not constitute a Christian life. Ministers must require more of their congregations; preachers must convince men that they were sinners and

---

[9] American Methodism owes its inspiration to George Whitefield, to the Wesleys, and to the Awakening; some of its congregations go back to the decades we have been discussing.

in danger; only then would worshippers seek assurance that they did, in truth, belong to God and not the devil.[10]

Ministers of less fervent temperament regarded Tennent's approach as an assault upon themselves. Antagonism was heightened by a kind of nationalistic rivalry, for the Tennent group were usually colonists by birth and education, whereas their antagonists, the men of the Old Side, as they were called, tended to be Scotch-Irishmen who had been trained in divinity in Scotland.

After five years of dispute, in 1741 the Old Side drove its opponents out of the Philadelphia Synod. The ousted Tennent group commanded much of the denomination's evangelical energy and popular appeal. It was they who succeeded in founding the College of New Jersey [11] (now known as Princeton) and it was they who won the most converts. Yet the very effectiveness of the Tennent group tended to change its character. The converts won to God by spiritual intensity had to be properly instructed, and the Tennent group found themselves becoming more and more involved with fostering interest in fine distinctions about the nature of repentance and the true love of God. So enthusiasm led, through education, to a denigration of enthusiasm, and the Awakening, which was so largely a rebellion against formalism in religion, gave rise to a new formalism.[12]

Before this occurred, however, the evangelical fervor of the Awakening carried Presbyterian preachers into new fields of activity. The success of their work encouraged,

[10] Leonard J. Trinterud, *Forming of an American Tradition* (Philadelphia: Westminster Press, 1949), p. 60.

[11] The Philadelphia Synod had jurisdiction over Presbyterian churches in New Jersey, where the Tennents had begun their work, and also in Virginia; this in part explains its importance.

[12] *See* Trinterud, *op. cit.*, p. 263.

indeed required them to initiate a new struggle for religious liberty in Virginia and also in New York, where tolerant Dutch rule had been succeeded by an English government which was more active in legislating on religious matters. In New York, however, efforts to check the proselytizing of Presbyterians and Baptists were part of a continuing struggle between the partisans of royal authority, generally Anglican in sympathy, and the partisans of autonomy, who were frequently Presbyterians. In Virginia the conflict appeared to be more clearly on the issue of freedom to preach without interference by the civil power.

Attempts to limit religious diversity and to maintain Anglican domination were not new in Virginia. In the early seventeenth century, Puritan settlers had been forced into more tolerant Maryland; later, Quakers were excluded from the colony and persecuted when they persisted in coming. Even after the English Toleration Act of 1689 allowed all dissenters freedom of worship (provided that they declared their allegiance to the king and their rejection of the Catholic doctrine of the real presence of God in the bread and wine of communion), the Governor and Council of Virginia continued to assert their right to arrest and punish evangelists who did not secure licenses to preach. And by and large, Presbyterians yielded to the civil power and applied for licenses, which were readily granted at this time.[13]

The conflict between Anglicans and Presbyterians in Virginia became more wordy after the Great Awakening had divided the Philadelphia Synod and the ousted Tennent

[13] Henry R. McIlwaine, "Struggle of Protestant Dissenters for Religious Toleration in Virginia" (Baltimore, Maryland: *Johns Hopkins University Studies in Historical and Political Science*, 1894), pp. 23, 28.

faction began to be active in the Valley of Virginia—the land between the Blue Ridge and the Alleghenies where Scotch-Irish Presbyterians were settling in considerable numbers. Although the licensing law never was strictly enforced, perhaps because of the difficulty of sending officers into the remote and hilly back country where it was easy to avoid pursuit, the Anglicans did fear that the fervent evangelism of the Presbyterian missionaries would win people away from the Established Church. Hence, during the early 1740's at least one grand jury inquired into the threat to public order arising from the activities of these missionaries and concluded that more rigorous enforcement of the laws was necessary; they called the Presbyterian evangelists "false teachers" who were deluding the ignorant.

Still, denied licenses though they might be, Presbyterian evangelists continued to come into the Valley, where their preaching was received, although we have record of at least one layman being fined for allowing an unlicensed minister to preach in his house.

After 1763, however, the Baptists became the primary object of Anglican antagonism. The Baptists [14] were conservative in theology—they believed in predestination—and fiercely separatist in church government, opposing most forms of cooperation among ministers and insisting that each church be composed of none but the saved who could be united on all points of doctrine. Baptist churches in America trace their origin to Roger Williams—it will be remembered how he opposed the authority of the synod in

[14] The relationship between this sect and European Anabaptists is obscure; it is not clear whether the English and American sects arose spontaneously or derived from Continental influence. Those called Anabaptists on the Continent held varying beliefs, but all seemed to have held in common the objection to infant baptism.

Massachusetts—and their relationship to the man they claim as founding father is shown in their consistent emphasis on separation between church and state.

Both the character of the Baptist constituency and the manner of its worship contributed to the hostility which Baptist evangelism aroused, particularly in Virginia. Rather frequently their ministers were laymen who felt the call to preach although they continued to earn their living as farmers and craftsmen. With warm earnestness, they urged men to repent and, hopefully, to attain conviction that they had been regenerated. The fact that these preachers, even if not laymen, were unlicensed was one reason for disapproval, for Baptist principles forbade preachers to ask for the legally required license to preach and evangelists were imprisoned for lack of a license, though none of the jail terms imposed was long. Conventional Anglicans also objected to the extreme enthusiasm of the Baptists, who made emotionalism the norm of worship rather than the exception marking a religious revival, and who often appealed to the poor; these felt alien in more formal congregations where preaching was learned and worship sober.

Still another reason for hostility was that the members of this sect refused to baptize infants. This provoked charges of cruelty, a not unjustified response since baptism was regarded as the necessary seal of Christian redemption —the unbaptized infant, if not condemned to hell, certainly could not join the saints in heaven. It must be remembered that at that time infant mortality was high; it has been estimated that 30 per cent of the infants born in the colonies died before they reached the age of five, long before they could have the kind of religious experience which Baptists thought would warrant the rite.

Opposition to Presbyterian activity tended to be official, whereas opposition to the Baptists in Virginia and farther south was often initially expressed in mob violence. When Samuel Harriss, a Baptist lay preacher, tried to speak in his native Pittsylvania County in the early 1760's, he was beaten and stoned. Other Baptist evangelists had similar experiences. Then officialdom used a logic not unfamiliar today; after the mob had acted, the authorities—county sheriffs and vestrymen—ordered the victims of the mobs arrested and jailed for disturbing the peace.

Mob violence against Baptist missionaries soon subsided, for their approach to religion actually answered a need and they won converts in increasing numbers. Baptist hostility to Virginia's established church never diminished. The Baptists particularly resented the possibility that marriages could be held invalid if performed by unlicensed ministers.

At the outbreak of the Revolutionary War, the Baptist community was all but unanimous in opposition to England. They expected separation from the British Empire to destroy their disabilities, along with Anglican privileges. The Presbyterians, too, generally supported the Revolution in the hope of gaining religious liberty. Thus the activity of the theologically conservative evangelists of the Awakening resulted in a struggle which gave rise to a degree of political radicalism. People who accepted a creed emphasizing the nothingness of man and all his works became partisans of man's capacity for self-government.

Neither the outbreak of the Revolution nor its success carried with it the change in policy which the non-Anglican groups demanded in Virginia. That change came only after an intensive political campaign which culminated in the adoption of the 1784 Statute for Religious Freedom. In

1799 came the final sign of disestablishment in Virginia: the glebe [15] lands of the Anglican Church were sold, thus ending public support for any religious organization in Virginia.

During the eighteenth century, religious life in the American colonies was affected by two currents: the Enlightenment and the Great Awakening. The first we have not discussed; it worked rather quietly and, by and large, among the upper classes. Not until the late 1780's and early 1800's do we see much evidence that men in the street were ready to doubt the inspiration of Scripture or to believe that human beings were sufficient unto their own spiritual redemption.

In the meantime, another movement toward belief in a different kind of evidence that salvation had been achieved was developing. The increase of churches and church membership gave the evangelist proof that in his sermons God had worked. In the prosperity of the community and its members, the laity saw evidence that they had received the Lord's grace. Worldly goods, once the Mammon of unrighteousness, were being transformed into testimony that righteousness had been achieved.

And however grace might operate—whether totally at the option of a wrathfully loving God or in response to sinners' beseeching—only diligence and shrewdness could win worldly gain.

[15] Lands set aside for the support of the church.

Order and Revolt   4

In Chapter 2, we encountered the Puritan problem: how to walk a middle way between antinomian [1] irresponsibility and rigid acceptance of formal belief. The colonial leaders of the movement against Britain's imperial policy faced a similar problem: how to walk a middle way between foreign rule and what was thought of as a threatened domestic anarchy.

In sketching the struggle for full religious liberty, we saw how Presbyterians and Baptists became hostile to what they regarded as pro-Anglican governments in New York and the Southern colonies, particularly in Virginia and Maryland. Although a few Baptists and some Presbyterians did take the loyalist side when conflict broke into warfare, still the need for support from religious dissidents in nominally Anglican colonies parallels the dilemma which men encountered during the crucial years between 1763 and 1789, when major political directions were determined.

Substantial merchants and planters in the colonies wanted to govern themselves in their own interests, not in the interest of the ruling class in Britain. Yet the substantial men of the colonies could not defend what they thought of as

[1] As we recall, the word *antinomian* was applied to those who believed that, since faith alone could save from sin, those who were certain that they had faith were not bound by the moral law.

their rights without help from the lower orders, the people or mob—the term chosen was apt to indicate one's politics. According to eighteenth-century standards, regular participation in politics by people who had little property was unseemly; independent political activity by those who had no property was dangerous. Many in power act as if they still believe that political capacity is proportional to property, but they do not often admit it. The eighteenth century was more forthright; it was apt to state its belief that a man's concern with the welfare of his country bore a direct relationship to the amount of that country he owned. The unpropertied were uneducated; they were unstable; they were untrustworthy, therefore, in anything but their own sphere. The mob had strong voices and strong arms, however. And the mob could be led. When led effectively, the mob was an excellent instrument with which to attack the *status quo*, especially since that was protected by so small an army as the British government had stationed in the mainland colonies. Still, the mob, roused, might not remain amenable to direction by its betters; it might make demands on its own account.

Compliance with those demands would mean anarchy, or so many leaders of what was to become a revolutionary movement maintained. When we consider the American Revolution, therefore, we should remember that many of its partisans felt they had taken a tiger by the tail. During the years before 1776, some Englishmen thought that this situation offered them a useful weapon in the struggle to preserve the empire. They hoped that, as their opponents saw how conflict with the mother country was forcing dependence on mob support, colonial men of property would pause, take thought, and turn tail in order to preserve their own local authority. And some leaders during the early period of resistance to British policy—the Presbyterian lawyer William Smith of New York, for example—did indeed change sides for just this reason.

The American Revolution and the decades which follow must be seen in the context of tension between desire for freedom from external control and desire to maintain a privileged position, between the rhetoric of natural rights and the reality of political power, between the declaration that most men are fit to govern themselves and the contention that most men are too corruptible to be entrusted with the task of government.

In 1763 all seemed well with the British Empire. Its long struggle for dominion had been won: the balance of power on the Continent had been maintained; Britain had defeated France in both America and India; British rule of the seas was assured. Nevertheless, even before the conclusion of the treaty of peace, warning voices were heard: France, defeated, would be plotting revenge; the peace accordingly should deprive her of all her possessions. Others were more cautious about stripping England's enemy. So long as the French held Canada, they contended, and continued friendly with the Indian tribes, the frontier settlements of the British mainland colonies stood threatened. So long as that threat was present, colonies would require British protection. The colonies, it was believed, would pay for that protection by complying with British regulations whenever the home government chose to enforce them. Britain should leave the frozen wastes of Canada to the French, therefore, and take Guadeloupe and Martinique as a more rewarding spoil of war.

Nevertheless, it was Canada, not Guadeloupe or Martinique, that was annexed. Scholars used to maintain that the "West India interest," the plantation owners and their spokesmen, exerted an exaggerated influence in Parliament, but close examination indicates that their lobbyists probably did not bar the acquisition of competing sugar-producing islands. Currently, historians lay greater emphasis on the influence of the great land companies which hoped to get grants and make profits out of the territory to be acquired. For Canada included not only the snowy deserts which Voltaire regarded as so trifling an object of contention, but also the rich lands of the "Illinois country," the northern part of the area between the Alleghenies and the Mississippi.

The land speculators had their way. The Peace of Paris of 1763 more than doubled Britain's holding in North America.

Until 1763, Britain had governed the mainland colonies by salutory neglect. It had rigid laws restricting colonial commerce, to be sure, but those laws were slackly enforced. It imposed political restraints, too, but they were often ignored. Certainly the colonial legislatures had taken control of the purse strings and so exerted enough political power to constitute a large measure of autonomy.

The newly enlarged empire called for firmer administration, the home government decided. Since reform would be costly and British property owners had been taxed heavily to pay for the wars just ended, it seemed reasonable that the mainland colonies should meet the costs of their own administration, costs which rose as territory to be guarded increased. The colonies were not expected to make any direct payment into the British Treasury, but they were to support a standing army, though they were to have no share in its staffing. More important, perhaps, the laws regulating colonial trade were now to be enforced, so that commerce would flow in the channels which brought the highest profit to British middlemen.

The new policy orientation was meant to restrain a people growing into what we may call a national consciousness. As Sir Henry Clinton observed—with the wisdom of hindsight and defeat—the British government undertook to make long-standing economic controls effective when "even the smallest innovation would . . . require the most experienced and cautious hand to direct it." [2]

The innovations which followed the Peace of Paris were not small; they came on the heels of irritating measures taken in 1759 and 1761, and they affected most of the politically active groups in the colonies. In 1759 there occurred a small but significant incident which grew in importance in the light of succeeding vexations. A newly adopted local Virginia law was disallowed, i.e., vetoed, by the Privy Council because the law had no provision delaying its operation until the Board of Trade—the contemporary equivalent of a Colonial Office—should have had time to consider the bill and, if it chose, to recommend disallowance to the Privy Council. Henceforth, formally, colonial legislatures could not legally make even local regulations effective until the long-drawn-out procedures of administration had been complied with.

Two years later, in 1761, the Board of Trade attempted to achieve indirectly what it had long sought to enforce as colonial policy, i.e., it attempted to trick colonial legisla-

<hr />

[2] William B. Willcox (ed.), *The American Rebellion: Sir Henry Clinton's Narratives of His Campaigns 1775-1782* (New Haven: Yale University Press, 1954), p. 1.

tures into making permanent provision for judicial officers —a measure the Board had long recommended as highly desirable, but which the colonial legislatures had no desire to accede to since, in so doing, they would make their judges independent of them (the power of the purse being dependent on the power to withhold funds). The Board of Trade attempted its maneuver now by appointing colonial judges for terms which might be ended "at the king's pleasure" rather than to serve "during good behavior," that is, for life. But, the honorable gentlemen announced blandly, if the colonial legislatures desired a judiciary completely independent of Britain, they could achieve that end at any time that they chose to comply with the suggestion that they make permanent provision for the salaries of court officers. The judiciary would then indeed be completely independent, both of Britain and the colonial legislatures.

The suggestion of the home government went unheeded, and colonial judges thenceforth sat on the bench at the king's pleasure. These measures and other administrative innovations of even more local application represented a latent threat to self-government; but it was the changes that came after the Peace of Paris which made the earlier changes seem significant.

Let us consider the impact of some of the new measures. First, the Proclamation Act of 1763 closed the lands newly acquired from France to speculators, unlicensed colonial Indian traders, and unauthorized settlers. The colonists read the law as an attempt to restrict their opportunities to expand, to profit, and to prosper. Their assumption seems to be borne out by the recommendation of the Board of Trade, which approved the Proclamation because it was

necessary to confine colonial settlement "to such a distance
from the seacoast as . . . should lie within the reach of the
trade and commerce of the kingdom. . . ." [3]

Ironically, however, the Proclamation Act was sponsored
by Lord Shelburne, then and later a friend of colonial
liberties, who intended the law as a mere stopgap until
Britain could develop a more coherent policy for dealing
with her new territories. This conflict of purpose between
Shelburne and his colleagues typified the conflict over
colonial policy which was to continue throughout the
1760's.

In 1763, also, a new policy of customs enforcement replaced long-standing administrative negligence. The Molasses Act of 1733, which levied a duty of 6d a gallon on
molasses from those West India islands which Britain did
not own, was replaced by a law cutting the duty to 3d a
gallon. This looks like a concession rather than an exaction,
until one realizes that compliant customs officers had earlier
devised ingenious ways to circumvent the old law: they
underestimated the quantity of dutiable cargo or even allowed a bribe to serve in lieu of duty payment. Colonial
merchants had paid only about 1d a gallon in duty, therefore, and colonial rum distilleries flourished as a result.

The law of 1763 not only lowered the duty but revised
regulations so that it would be collected. Local customs
officers now had to post bonds and keep detailed records;
they could underestimate cargo or allow nonpayment of
duty only by risking forfeiture of their bonds. Furthermore,
in order to check smuggling, the British Navy was now to
patrol the American coast line. Since officers and men

[3] Bernard Knollenberg, *Origin of the American Revolution 1759-1766*
(New York: The Macmillan Co., 1960), p. 104.

shared in the proceeds when confiscated smuggled cargoes
were sold, they were apt to be earnest in enforcing the law.
As a further hindrance to smuggling, the many small
farmers and traders, who moved their goods by water in
those days of poor roads, were now required to comply
with the formalities of clearance even if they were merely
carrying vegetables from Long Island to Connecticut.

The following year, 1764, colonial uneasiness was sharpened by further legislation. The colonies were forbidden to
issue paper money. (Colonial issues already in circulation
were not required to be withdrawn.) Previously, royal disallowance had been used to forbid particular colonies from
printing paper money; the prohibition was now made general, a matter of law, not of administrative policy. Parliament regarded the new law as no more than decent
protection for British creditors. To colonial businessmen
and landowners, the ban on new paper currency issues
seemed designed to restrict their enterprise. Little capital
accumulated in the colonies: what the colonists sold brought
less than what they bought in England and the consequent
adverse trade balance drained away hard money. As has
been said, there were no mines in the colonies to make
good that loss. Nor were there any banks. Hence, bank
credit and checks could not be used to supplement or replace currency. Paper money was the colonists' only alternative to barter. The alternative was perilous, to be
sure: when the printing press is used to produce cash, without the backing of specie, the temptation to overproduce
is all but irresistible. And British creditors had no stomach
for payment in depreciated paper money.

The innovations in British policy did not affect only the
more prosperous groups in the colonies. As if determined

to give all elements fresh grievances, the government au-
thorized measures which seemed almost calculated to bring
the colonial mob into the streets. British vessels of war
attempted to impress colonial seamen. When the Navy
needed hands, it had the legal right to impress sailors from
fishing vessels and merchant ships and it extended that right,
scouring the waterfront and impressing any able-bodied
man who, it could be claimed, might be a sailor. But when
the Navy tried to impress men in Newport and New York,
mobs rescued the sailors. Their success—for no one was
prosecuted—showed how effectively violence could prevent
the enforcement of unpopular laws in the colonies.

In 1765 Parliament adopted a measure which particularly
irritated the laboring classes, especially in New York. This
was the well-known Quartering Act. The law provided
that, as in England, when troops were sent to areas where
no barracks were available, soldiers might be quartered in
barns and similar outbuildings. Furthermore—and this was
not demanded in towns in England where troops were stationed—the colonies were required to provide soldiers with
straw, candles, firewood, and vinegar (this last as an anti-
scorbutic). The New York legislature refused to obey
(New York was now the headquarters for the British Army
in North America) and the legislature was suspended, an
act which won it support from people who generally had
no votes but who could and did provide effective manpower
for turbulent political protest.

In the eighteenth century, the men who served in the
ranks of England's small standing army—volunteers paid
6d a day, less deductions, and compelled to serve no less
than twelve years—were not regarded as heroes. As Mrs.
Mercy Warren, the first American woman to write history,

put it: wherever part of a standing army might be quartered ". . . it introduces a revolution in manners, corrupts the morals, propagates every species of vice, and degrades the human character." [4]

The longshoremen and porters and carters of New York and Boston used less elegant language than Mrs. Warren, but their opinion of British soldiers was no more flattering. The enmity between the casual laborers, the journeymen mechanics, and the "lobsterbacks"—the British soldiers who were allowed to compete with them for jobs—provided an appropriate setting for the urban violence which characterizes the thirteen years before the Revolution. That period, incidentally, opened during something of a depression; peace with France meant not only the end of military spending in the mainland colonies, but also of opportunities for trading with the enemy, because during peacetime, the French excluded from their West Indian ports the English colonial vessels whose cargoes were so useful in time of war. Accordingly, although trade with the British and Spanish West Indies continued, the profits of merchants declined and opportunities for employment diminished.

When Parliament proposed a Stamp Act in 1765, many colonial leaders regarded the law as an unbearable imposition. For the Act required that wills, contracts, deeds, licenses, and the many documents needed by shippers (as well as newspapers, advertisements, dice, and playing cards) bear stamps which had to be paid for in hard money—not the paper money still in circulation in the colonies—and at rather high rates. At the same time, by stricter enforcement of the laws controlling colonial trade, the new British policy

[4]Mercy Warren, *History of the Rise, Progress and Termination of the American Revolution*, Vol. I (Boston, 1805), p. 62.

cut the colonies off from their principal opportunity to get gold and silver for their fish, grain, flour, and lumber.

Such a burdening of trade, with the Spanish West Indies particularly, seems to run counter to one tenet of mercantilist orthodoxy—the more specie one brought into the state the better—since it blocked an opportunity to acquire specie from a foreign enemy. This contradiction seemed to have attracted relatively little attention, however. The eighteenth century tended to cast its arguments on political policy in legal and constitutional terms rather than in terms of economic prudence.

Nevertheless, in 1764-65, while the Stamp Act was pending, most colonial leaders would have regarded arguments in favor of independence as an evil fantasy. Those same leaders, however, were all but unanimous in opposition to the Stamp Act. Indeed, the list of those who made formal protest against the proposed law has a number of names in common with those on lists of later Loyalists, men who lost their property because they continued faithful to Crown and Empire. One might indeed study the crucial years between the Stamp Act Congress and the Declaration of Independence in terms of the movements of political leaders toward either end of the scale between capitulation to parliamentary supremacy and the hazards of independence.

That polarizing movement had scarcely begun when news that Parliament indeed meant to adopt the Stamp Act came to the colonies. In the resistance to the law, however, one can see more than hints of political methods and conflicts to come. The first colonial protest came through the colonial agents—official lobbyists in London, generally instructed by their legislatures—and then, when the law was actually adopted, from the legislatures directly. New York took the strongest stand, for although it accepted Parliament's right to regulate colonial trade, the New York legislature denied that Parliament had any right to tax the colonies, either externally, by way of duties on imported merchandise, or internally, by way of excises like the Stamp Act itself. Rhode Island was first to suggest formally that the colonies send delegates to a conference for joint action. When Parliament disregarded protests, the colonists held their conference. Only five colonies actually sent delegates to the Stamp Act Congress, which met at New York, and that body did no more than draft a petition for repeal of the law.

There was also more forcible action. Stamp collectors were burned in effigy—a hint to resign which most of them accepted. The stamps themselves were destroyed or seized, except when the authorities succeeded in hiding them from the mob; in any case, they were never used. Some newspapers suspended publication. Others were printed on unstamped paper. Cards were marketed without stamps on the packages. Some courts carried on, although there was no stamped paper for documents. Other courts closed, much to the pleasure of debtors whose mortgages could not be foreclosed in due form.

The colonies were in actual rebellion in 1765; and that rebellion achieved its end: the Grenville Ministry was replaced by a cabinet committed to repeal of the Stamp Act. But success in getting rid of the law roused the leaders of the colonial opposition to uneasy awareness that they were bringing new factors into the political arena. We should remember that every man with any pretension to education knew something about the history of Rome and thought

he knew what disorder and terror necessarily entered public life when the lower classes were allowed an effective
voice in it. And the lower classes had helped procure the
repeal of the Stamp Act.

Because of this rising concern, one can see, in most colonies, the development of at least three active factions. One
faction was ultimately to become the Loyalists; these people
soon turned to full-scale opposition to attacks on British
policy. A second faction—which will be referred to as the
Revolutionary moderates—continued in opposition, but
tried to act with minimal concession to the lower classes.
The third faction—whom we shall call the Revolutionary
radicals—was willing to push opposition with whatever
allies might be effective.

Conservatives and moderates might have composed their
differences and controlled the situation in the colonies had
British policy reverted to at least a measure of that slackness
of administration which had brought prosperity to the
mainland colonies and profit to England. The intricacies of
British politics in a transition age cannot be dealt with here,
of course, but we should note that colonial policy was
linked with the effort of Tory factions in England to replace the Whig factions which had ruled so long. These
Tories argued that the colonies should pay for their own
defense and civil service. The colonists, they said, had no
reason to complain about efforts to raise a revenue among
them because the money would be spent in America. In
opposition, some of the Whig factions believed, with Edmund Burke who first used the phrase, that continued "salutory neglect" would mean continued and increasing profit
for England. Effort to raise a revenue in the colonies would
merely make a politically sensitive people more tender of

its rights. Ideological disputation would make for emotional involvement, in our phrase, and that involvement, Burke argued, would make rational compromise impossible.

And so it was to be.

Not, however, before a series of British measures evoked colonial countermeasures which sharpened the political paradox: most prudent men agreed with the Puritan leaders cited in Chapter 2: that democracy was the worst form of government. Many prudent men, nevertheless, found it necessary to use democratic instruments to protect the rights which they claimed as Englishmen, and therefore as members of a hierarchically organized society

During the first phase of conflict, as we have shown, petitions reinforced by local mob violence had persuaded British politicians, already opposed to the measure, to repeal the Stamp Act. For reasons primarily connected with British issues, this group of Whigs (the Rockingham faction) was forced out of office by a rival group, whose most important figure was Charles Townshend. Under his leadership, Parliament adopted new laws which taxed goods imported into the colonies. Because these were duties on imports and not an excise like the Stamp Act, Townshend and his followers argued that the British government was respecting the colonists' distinction between external taxes, which they accepted as within Parliament's authority, and internal levies, which they declared constituted taxation without representation.

The colonial opposition abandoned its original position and, with bland inconsistency, shifted ground and declared that the new taxes were to be judged by their purpose not their form. It took new countermeasures, including formal agreement to boycott British goods until the law should be changed. The moderates recognized the dangers latent in this sort of resistance, for an effective boycott required the great merchants, who had most to lose, to cooperate not only with less important merchants but even with artisans and the laborers on the waterfront who were in a good position to see whether promises not to import were being kept.

Jonathan Boucher, Anglican minister, anti-Whig propagandist, and finally Loyalist refugee, put it pithily when he said that boycotts were fundamentally evil because enforcing them gave the poor power to harass their richer neighbors.[5] The moderate colonial opposition may well have agreed with him; certainly the moderates were relieved when repeal of the Townshend duties of 1767 gave reason for a pause in the conflict. To be sure, Parliament formally asserted its power to tax the colonies under any circumstances it chose, and Parliament continued the import duty on tea. But the moderates drank smuggled tea when they could and treated Parliament's declaration as so much wind.

Agitation subsided. The more passionate exponents of colonial rights regarded the moderates as backsliders, ready to surrender liberty for a mess of pottage, but their viewpoint won little support. Then, in 1773, the British government rescued the intransigents. By that time, a new kind of hostility to the colonists had appeared in England. The success of colonial boycotts in forcing a change of policy had roused uneasiness. The shift of colonial argument had wakened further distrust, for the colonists had given up the logically untenable distinction between internal and external taxes which Charles Townshend had so lucklessly

---

[5] Jonathan Boucher, *Causes and Consequences of the American Revolution* (London, 1797), p. xlvi.

recognized. Would the colonists not soon shift ground again, it was asked; would they not repudiate their proclaimed loyalty to the imperial system and proclaim their natural right to trade as they wished, sending goods where they fetched the highest price, buying in the cheapest market, and keeping middlemen's profits in colonial ports instead of in the pockets of British factors, shippers, and other intermediaries? Furthermore, ever present as a potential consequence of colonial refusal to import British goods was the possibility that the colonists, if not soon and firmly checked, would respond to the boycotters' urging that domestic products be used and turn to manufacturing for themselves.

Thus, latent hostility sharpened. The English political climate, moreover, had changed from what it was in 1768. By 1772, when Parliament adopted the Tea Act, the so-called King's Friends—led by Lord North, a group neither wholly Whig nor Tory in the traditional sense—had a fairly firm grasp on the House of Commons. The Tea Act actually reduced the tax on tea, but it gave the East India Company exclusive rights to market tea in the colonies. Lowering the tax would make tea smuggling less profitable; this pleased many colonial moderates, who disliked disorder even when they themselves were responsible for it. Even to these moderates, however, the approach to a monopoly in the marketing of tea seemed a threat both to liberty and to property. Conscientiously moderate colonials felt insulted as well as betrayed by the new turn in British policy; ineptitude of this sort, they assumed, had to be deliberate. To colonial moderates, British policy was obviously playing into the hands of the radical leaders, if not of the rabble itself. For, until 1773, the partisans of continued economic pressure on Britain had been losing ground in every colony. Word of the Tea Act brought former allies together again. The mob seemed less fearsome to ". . . the more judicious and discreet characters" [6] than the consequences of giving monopoly a foothold. Once again, therefore, boycott and violence were brought into play as political instruments.

British reaction in 1774-75 was different from what it had been in 1765-66. After the Boston Tea Party (tea was destroyed in other cities, incidentally), Parliament closed the port of Boston and all but destroyed the autonomy which Massachusetts had long enjoyed. The colonies replied by calling a Continental Congress. Parliament ignored the petition of this irregular body and defeated motions for conciliation. Then came Lexington and Concord, and war was recognized as inevitable by both sides. It is not our purpose to describe the Revolution here, nor is it our purpose to account for its outcome. But in the development of that struggle we may see a curious likeness between those who opposed the colonial cause and some of those who, like Gouverneur Morris, supported it. Many of the latter held significant positions in the government set up in 1789. Knowledge of their attitudes contributes to understanding some of the paradoxes implicit in American political ideas and practices.

Because New York was so centrally situated and because even in the eighteenth century its population was relatively cosmopolitan (though perhaps rather less so than contemporary Pennsylvania), the Province of New York presents an instructively complex picture during the Revolutionary era. Its geographical position gave it great military importance. New York's large Loyalist faction contributed

6 Warren, *op. cit.*, 1:30.

materially to British fighting power (and perhaps to British misconceptions about the nature of the task they had to face). Consequently, the likeness between the attitude of Judge Thomas Jones, disappointed New York Loyalist, and Gouverneur Morris, realistically conservative New York Whig, is peculiarly pertinent. The Judge describes New York as a truly happy community in 1752.[7] Then came William Livingston, that "shrewd, morose, bigoted, uncouth, cruel, wanton, oily hypocrite" and William Smith, educated at Yale, ". . . then and still a nursery of sedition, of faction, and of republicanism." [8] Livingston and Smith, together with John Morin Scott, and John Lamb, whose father was a reformed highwayman, joined the Whig Club which, Jones said, devoted itself to drinking toasts to Cromwell and planning to pull down the church, ruin the constitution, and "heave the whole province into confusion."

The Stamp Act, said the Judge, gave this triumvirate its opportunity: "Mobs were raised and encouraged by gentlemen of the first ranks." People whom even the Judge considered respectable, James Duane and John Jay, for example, went on to "fabricate" an association claiming "to prevent mobs, to support the civil authority," and actually to defend the "rights and liberties of the people" against ministry and Parliament.[9]

If Tory Judge Jones saw the rising Whigs thus acidly, Whig Gouverneur Morris saw them in no more glowing a light. Thus, writing of the Committees of Correspondence, Morris said: "The heads of the mobility grow dangerous

[7] Thomas Jones, *History of New York*, Vol. I (New York: New York Historical Society, 1879), p. 1.

[8] Ibid., I, 3; 31-33.

[9] Ibid., I, 6; 42.

to the gentry, and how to keep them down is the question." [10] As late as 1774, Morris continued to be distressed:

> [Reunion is essential to both countries.] It is for the interest of all men to seek reunion with the parent State. The spirit of the English constitution has yet a little influence left, and but a little. The remains of it will give the wealthy people a superiority, but would they secure it, they must banish all school masters and confine all knowledge to themselves. This cannot be—the mob begin to think—the gentry begin to fear this—their committee [to enforce non-importation] will be appointed—they will deceive the people and again forfeit a share of their confidence. And if these are instances of what with one side is policy, with the other perfidy, farewell aristocracy. I see, and I see it with fear and trembling, that if the disputes with Britain continue, we shall be under the worst of all possible dominions, the dominion of a riotous mob. [11]

Yet when, in 1776, Britain did send commissioners to try to procure reunion (a general and an admiral in command of armed forces at their head), Morris said he would be more ready to trust "crocodiles" than his Majesty's Commissioners. [12]

Many Revolutionary moderates, then, were forced to live in conflict between the need to maintain social order, which often meant their own power, and the need to establish that power by carrying the revolution to victory—a goal to be achieved only with the assistance of the Revolutionary radicals. Like the moderates, the radicals distrusted human nature: all men were basically "kittle cattle," unreliable, brutal, easily duped, prone to run after innovations. But the

[10] M. B. Macmillan, *War Governors in the American Revolution* (New York: Columbia University Press, 1842), p. 18.

[11] Ann Cary Morris (ed.), *Diary and Letters of Gouverneur Morris*, Vol. I (New York: Charles Scribner's Sons, 1888), p. 4.

[12] Ibid., I, 6.

radicals considered the ruling class to be as human as the rest of mankind. If all men had a potential for evil, as well as some potential for good, then all men and all groups of men were potential tyrants and oppressors.

Democracy is usually thought of as an optimistic philosophy of government. As expounded by its partisans in the eighteenth century, democracy actually expressed a thoroughgoing belief in political depravity. Because all men were of such a nature that no man could safely be trusted with any but the most limited degree of power over other men, government had to be based on legally limited institutions so balanced as to offset each other's range of actions. Thus, it would become impossible for any person or group of persons to concentrate political power in itself.

Note that in their analysis of the problem of political power, the Revolutionary radicals, like the Revolutionary moderates, were not unaware of the relationship between the two power spheres: economic and political. Indeed, both groups saw some of the roots of despotism, of uncontrolled governmental power, in the struggle between the "haves" and the "have nots." Always in the past, some men had been shrewd or strong enough to acquire a disproportionate amount of wealth; and, if given the chance, the rest had banded together to take that wealth away from them. Such bands had generally broken up in struggle over the division of the spoils. As an alternative to the ensuing anarchy, the possessors of wealth had promoted tyranny— first in its classic sense of rule by a man who had no hereditary claim to his position, and then in governments with almost untrammeled powers. The non-possessors had acquiesced: oppression which provided some order was more tolerable than no order at all. Nevertheless, even oppressive government with powers unlimited by law depended upon some "consent" by the governed; against governments which exceeded a certain measure of oppression, even the acquiescent would rise.

To be sure, the most successful risings—movements which had effectively limited governments—had occurred in countries where the people were relatively well off. The continuing revolution which turned England into eighteenth-century Europe's prime example of the distribution of political power began in the 1640's, when England still enjoyed a large measure of that prosperity she had known under the Tudors. The revolutionary leaders in Parliament beheaded one king and only a generation later, after the restoration of the Stuarts, forced the abdication of another, and limited the power of succeeding monarchs.

Roman and English experience were much in the minds of the American Revolutionary leaders. For them, the study of history was more than an agreeable diversion or an exercise in research. Men could actually learn from the past, they believed. Although they might not agree on the content of the lessons which history taught, all agreed that history had lessons to teach.

One of these lessons was the influence of passion on judgment. In Madison's words: "As long as the reason of man continues fallible . . . As long as the connection subsists between his reason and his self-love, his opinions and his passions will have a reciprocal influence on each other; and the former will be objects to which the latter will attach themselves." [13]

Like woman in the poem, the people were "uncertain, coy, and hard to please." But so were their betters. Since

[13] *Federalist* (New York: Colonial Press, 1901), p. 45.

power was least dangerous when most diffused, rule by the people was the safest form of government. The best man might be corrupted; the wisest man might play the fool; aristocracies might deteriorate. But inevitable corruption and folly could do their worst only when joined to far-ranging and unrestrained political power.

On the whole, the Revolutionary leadership accepted these premises; differences came at the point of operation. How much power in government was "too" much? How was salutory and necessary diffusion of power to be combined with, and balanced against, the concentration of power necessary to give the newly independent nation at least a tolerably respectable position in the world?

A respectable nation maintains its authority against violation of its rights by foreigners and against disorderly persons within its boundaries; it pays its debts. Measured by these yardsticks, the United States was not respectable between 1783 and 1789. It was not able to force Britain to keep the terms of the Treaty of 1783 which pledged that nation to surrender its military posts in what is now Michigan and Illinois, and also to pay for slaves lost to the Southerners during the course of the war. It was not paying its debts, foreign or domestic, and there were internal disorders. Discontent among those suffering from postwar economic dislocation was expressing itself in laws which sought to force depreciated paper money into circulation at face value, and laws which sought to protect debtors against their creditors. When such laws could not be obtained (as in doggedly respectable Massachusetts), discontent expressed itself in violence, as typified in Shays' Rebellion.

With the outbreak of that insurrection in 1786, the need for national respectability became evident even to people who had thus far found the loose federation provided by the Articles of Confederation to be a tolerable form of government. That instrument, incidentally, provided for common citizenship and mutual acceptance of each state's legal proceedings. What the Articles made no provision for was an independent source of revenue which would enable the United States to pay its debts and to maintain the military force that would bring Britishers and insurgents to proper regard for the rights of the nation and to decent respect for order.

Some historians have argued that partisans of a central government more powerful than that provided in the Articles exaggerated the threat implicit in Shays' Rebellion in order to give a sharp object lesson to those who were insufficiently aware of the nation's weakness.[14] The *coup d'état* theory of the Constitution, which was explicitly formulated by J. Allen Smith and Charles Beard, is no longer fashionable. Be that as it may, it is clear that the political impotence of the United States most affected the politically and economically energetic groups in the new country. These were the people who sponsored the commercial conventions that finally led to the Constitutional Convention. And these were the people who got the new Constitution ratified. They gained control of the new government and with that control established a financial policy that made the United States respectable.

Although the Federalists were successful as administrators and as formulators of policy, they were unsuccessful in the art of securing political power. The impractical Jeffersonians drove their practical opponents out of office. Never-

[14] Richard B. Morris (ed.), *Era of the American Revolution* (New York: Columbia University Press, 1930).

theless, once in office, the Jeffersonians not only continued
the financial program they had first opposed, but even, as
we shall see in the next chapter, were forced to revive the
national bank whose founding they had so strongly and so
futilely fought.

Contrasting the Federalists and the Jeffersonians merely
in regard to their opinion of man, one can say that the
Jeffersonians put as much trust in the ordinary man as in
elites, whereas the more optimistic Federalists thought elite
rule was necessary. In a country where acceptance of such
rule was not a matter of course—and increasingly the
United States was becoming such a country—it was necessary to beguile ordinary men into accepting rule by their
betters. In 1802 Hamilton recognized this when he sketched
a method for winning the common man to Federalism. The
Christian Constitutional Society, which he proposed in a
letter to Thomas Bayard, with its emphasis on religion and
order, would seem congenial to many a contemporary conservative. On the whole, however, Hamilton seems handicapped by knowledge that he was talking cant.

In the main, John Adams agreed with Hamilton's point
of view regarding the elite and the mob, but he disliked the
prospect of an aristocracy based on the command of credit.
Pessimistically, he told his old opponent, Jefferson—both
men were writing in 1813, long after the passions of political
rivalry had ebbed—that "birth and wealth together have
prevailed over virtue and talent in all ages." Aristocracies,
he said, were inevitable, since nature was not even-handed
in giving men "beauty, wealth, birth, genius, but was per-
force content with rule by the rich, the well-born and the
able."

Jefferson agreed with Adams in regard to the lack of

equality of gifts among men, but Jefferson emphasized that
wealth and birth were hallmarks of the "mischievous" arti-
ficial aristocracy he deplored; natural aristocracy—talent
and virtue—was "the most precious gift of nature" and that
constitution was best which best provided for bringing
such people into government. Before ". . . the establishment of the American States, nothing was known to history
but the man of the old world, crowded into limits either
small or over-charged, and steeped in the vices which that
situation generates." [15]

Once again, we see the hard-bitten concepts of human
nature which underlie what has been called Jeffersonian
optimism. Men in favorable circumstances, Jefferson
thought, and in those only (". . . the *canaille* of the cities
of Europe would be instantly perverted to the demolition
and destruction of everything, public and private . . ."),
could be trusted to "select the able and good for the direction of their government" and frequent elections would
permit the ousting of "an unfaithful servant before the
mischief he meditates may be irredeemable." [16]

Many years earlier, as Jonathan Boucher expounded the
damage which the American Revolution had done, he said:
"The strength and efficacy" of religion and government
depend "on the persuasion that they [religion and govern-
ment] are already perfect." [17] By their actions, the Founding Fathers denied this. They not only broke away from an
established government, they justified their action by arguing that governments are instituted by men for visible human purposes. They asserted, too, that men might judge

[15] Paul Wilstach (ed.) *Correspondence of John Adams and Thomas
Jefferson* (Indianapolis, Ind.: Bobbs-Merrill, 1925), p. 93.
[16] Ibid., p. 95.
[17] Jonathan Boucher, *op. cit.,* p. 203.

whether their own governments were fulfilling the purposes for which all governments were established. The American Republic thus took its stand on the principle that institutions had no prescriptive rights. Whatever existed had to demonstrate—or at least plausibly defend—its right to be.

In this fashion, what we may call the "philosophy" of American government allowed no American group (except perhaps the slaveholding upper class of the Tidewater South) to develop the kind of security which an aristocratic society fosters in its elites. Ruling groups in the United States—when they inadvertently reveal themselves as such—cannot rest their right to govern on unquestioned authority. Their rule must show justifying success. No American elite can inherit the expectation of deference, political as well as social, which has been the birthright of traditional aristocracies.

Such a demand for demonstrated effectiveness cuts the ground from under classic conservatism in the United States. For true conservatism asserts that an orderly society depends on acceptance of the rule that certain aspects of the social world stand beyond objective scrutiny. Once men scrutinize any laws, their natural depravity and rebelliousness will make all civil peace impossible. Among the laws which the conservatives insist stand like those of the Medes and the Persians is the the supremacy of the governors. When this is denied, when any group, call itself what it may, feels obliged to legitimatize its claims by pointing to tangible benefits, such unquestioning acceptance of its leadership is not possible.

The American Revolution has been called incomplete because it did not truly alter the structure of power. In many respects, this contention is valid. Nevertheless, by basing government's right to exist upon performance, and by claiming for all men the right to examine that performance, the American Revolution was by far a greater threat to all "establishments" than subsequent political developments would suggest.

Freeing the Field 5

THE REVOLUTIONARY MODERATES feared two things: if men of lesser means were active in politics, the legislatures they elected would plunder the rich; and if political influence were in the hands of "the lower orders," to use the eighteenth-century phrase, it would operate to encourage idleness. Further, during the early years of the Republic, it was held that if wages were high and land relatively easy to obtain, men would get their living easily; they would not work hard enough to produce much surplus, and the nation would not accumulate wealth.

Time proved all these fears to be unwarranted. No state legislature, however popularly elected, acted to transfer money from the pockets of the rich to the pockets of the poor.[1] And Americans soon acquired a reputation for bitter dedication to making money.

One may see the political struggle of the ensuing period— that is between 1789 and 1812, particularly—as a clash of national purposes: the pursuit of national wealth as against the pursuit of individual happiness. As that clash proceeded, the Jeffersonians, opponents of governmental action to

[1] Unless the repudiation of debts by certain states in the 1830's be counted as such a transfer. The rich thus affected were foreigners, Englishmen mostly, who had thought themselves safe as creditors of such states as Pennsylvania.

speed economic growth, were forced to take measures
which most effectively furthered their opponents' objectives. It is their dilemma and the consequences of its resolution which form the subject of this chapter. For it was
the Jeffersonians who, by cutting off imports (as part of the
measures to avoid conflict with France and England over
the impressment of seamen and the seizure of ships and
cargoes), gave American industry possession of the American market, an insurance of profit far more effective than
the scheme of subsidies and tariffs which Hamilton had
planned and failed to achieve in the 1790's.

By 1791 Hamilton had carried his project for setting up
a national bank, having first re-funded the Federal and
State debts. The debts were money originally owed by the
Continental Congress and by the states to creditors, foreign
and domestic, and to soldiers of the Continental Army. The
new government, following Hamilton's plan, took over
these debts at face value, guaranteeing payment by issuing
bonds and providing that interest and principal be paid out
of government revenues. Being guaranteed by government
revenue, the new bonds were considered a good investment
and hence could be used as collateral in borrowing from
banks. Thus, in effect, public debt was converted into a
substitute for capital; it augmented the money supply and
eased credit, for business. Meanwhile, the national bank
which had been set up served as an efficient lending agency
and, by its ability to demand redemption of other banks'
notes, also served as a check upon overinflationary issues of
currency by lesser banks.[2] With a capital substitute avail-

[2] These were private banks under state charter. The national bank,
too, was a private bank, having a charter from the Federal government
which owned some of its stock and appointed a number of persons to
represent its interest on the bank's board of directors. (These, however,

able, anticipated profits could be drawn upon in advance. Men would borrow to undertake new enterprises; if those succeeded, they would create tangible wealth as well as speculative fortunes, and the nation would prosper.

For the kind of prosperity which meant national power, however, it was not sufficient that public credit be firm enough to support commercial ventures; it was necessary that the economy be diversified, that manufacturing be developed. Since land speculation and commerce gave enterprising men high returns, only still higher returns, coupled with a measure of security, could encourage them to risk investment in industry. Consequently, Hamilton concluded that Congress should adopt a system of protection which stressed short-term bounties as well as protective duties.

Cogently though Hamilton argued for his program, it was never adopted. The opposition, at first overwhelmed by the early superior organization, efficiency, and discipline of Hamilton's supporters, finally rallied and defeated his program for industry.

That defeat occurred the more readily because Hamilton's own backers were not single-minded in support of all his measures. He was an uncomfortably brilliant leader. His followers agreed with his political philosophy: most men were incapable of self-government, personal or political. But a number of Hamilton's followers were disquieted by certain parts of his economic program. Particularly, they were not ready to accept his plans for forcing economic diversification (in the sense that hothouse plants are forced).

took very little part in the operation of the bank.) The bank might do business in any state and enjoyed a monopoly of the right to act as Federal financial agent, transacting government business and holding government funds on deposit.

Revolutionary moderate Gouverneur Morris, friend and co-worker of Hamilton though he had been, was only one follower who boggled at accepting the whole of Hamilton's scheme. It was well, Morris thought, that the national credit should be established. It was well, too, that a national bank be available to serve the government's financial needs and to lend merchants money. But as for protective tariffs—in Morris' opinion, the gentleman who hired men to build a stone wall about his estate contributed far more to national respectability than did the man who took advantage of tariff protection to start a factory and encourage the scum of England and Ireland to come and "batten" upon American farmers.

In rejection of Hamilton's program, Revolutionary moderate and Revolutionary radical approached each other in a genuinely conservative opposition to measures which would create a basic change in the country.

Here, John Taylor of Caroline,[3] Senator from Virginia, anticipated Morris by several years. Agriculture, Taylor argued, was the one true foundation of national felicity. Other economic activity had only dubious value. "Dealing in paper," as Taylor labeled credit transactions, was of no value at all. For the tangibles produced by farming and necessary manufacture, the Hamiltonians would substitute a feverish circulation of credit. This might stimulate the economy, Taylor admitted, but stimulants were as dangerous to the body politic as to the body physical. Certainly,

[3] Between the middle 1700's and the 1830's, Virginia echoes this much of European aristocracy: certain important families—the Randolphs, the Taylors, and the Carters, for example—were so prolific, and so unimaginative in the choice of Christian names, that their members were distinguished by the name of the county or the plantation where they lived.

the Hamiltonian program would force an economic development which would come, Taylor said, albeit more slowly, without encouragement—and which was likely to produce little good when it did come.

In John Taylor's battle against Hamilton's policies, we have, too, an expression of the philosophy so frequently held in the decades just after the Revolution: the good life of men in the new republic was only a temporary blessing. Human experience, as recorded in history—and reading history was then a favorite diversion of American statesmen—showed that free governments could exist only in a special situation, namely, abundant land and a relatively simple way of life. That situation was by nature impermanent. The United States had been peculiarly favored. It was politically sinful to cast its natural blessings aside, to give governmental encouragement to the development of a complex economy and so speed a free republic's inevitable decay into plutocracy and tyranny.

Yet, ironically, as we have said, the foreign policy favored by people like John Taylor himself operated to the end they opposed. In the 1790's Senator Taylor was among those who voted for discriminatory taxes on British commerce in an attempt to force that nation to pay for "kidnapped" American slaves and to give more liberal treatment to American shipping. (This would mean a bigger market for Virginia wheat, incidentally.) Hamilton opposed this course of action vehemently and successfully: discrimination would evoke retaliation; furthermore, any drop in imports from the most important of the United States' trading partners would cut off the customs revenue which was the chief source of Federal revenue and the basis of the Treasury's ability to maintain public credit by paying interest on the public debt. In order to carry through one part of his program, Hamilton was forced to oppose an efficient although risky method of realizing another, that is, excluding that British competition which was the major check on the development of American industry. Long after Hamilton's death, those who had once accepted his leadership continued to oppose the anti-British measures of the dominant faction among the Jeffersonians. And many among the Jeffersonians, in their turn, supported anti-British policies even though those operated to further an end most of them deplored, that is, a forcing of economic growth and diversification.

In the end, after more than a decade of effort to avoid battle, the United States found itself at war with Britain. It was after the War of 1812, into which expansionist desires forced Madison's administration, that the followers of Jefferson's philosophy realized the need for a national bank, particularly in order to finance war, and, wise after the event, chartered the Second Bank of the United States.

The War of 1812 gave great stimulus to textile manufacture in America. It also had a major impact on other phases of industry. Eli Whitney is known to every school child as the inventor of the cotton gin. Eli Whitney, as a successful developer of the concept of interchangeable parts, is less well known. It was he who seems first to have applied what appears like the simple and inevitable idea of making the parts of objects—muskets in this instance—so much alike that one could be substituted for another. War, with its increased demand for guns, gave impetus to the adoption of the new method, which was soon used in other industries, notably clock and watchmaking. The nation did not cease to import machine tools—or textiles, for that

matter—after 1812, but the ground had been prepared for
the development of the complex economy which the Hamiltonian partisans of national power had desired to speed
and whose coming their opponents wished to postpone.

In the growth of this complex economy, one finds the
roots of the social ferment, the intellectual hopes and dis-
quiets, which give such sharp color to the three decades
before the Civil War. The American manner had changed.
Peter Kalm, the Swedish naturalist who visited the American colonies in the 1740's, described Americans as a loung-
ing people, idle and gossiping. John Bernard, the English
actor, saw them as much the same after the Revolution.
English Chartist Thomas Brothers, emigrated in the 1830's
because he saw no chance for the political reforms which
he thought England needed. Years of work as a hatmaker in
Philadelphia cured Brothers of his attachment to democracy, he said; and nothing in his experience had been more
medicinal than the speed and effort which were demanded
of American workers. No Englishman would endure being
driven in that fashion.

Brothers is confirmed, in a way, by Jedidiah Allen, industrialist of Rhode Island who visited England in the early
1830's and was vividly struck by the English workman's
resistance to new methods and the indifference to improvement which even the more intelligent among them displayed. A sufficiency of beer and tobacco seemed all their
aim; they neither aspired nor accumulated.

The industrial change which Allen saw as so whole-
heartedly welcomed by his countrymen had hazards which
Allen and his like tended less to ignore than to discount.
Among these hazards one might count the consequences of
movement away from rural areas and into cities. The move-

ment was not the dominant note of American life before the Civil War, to be sure, but it was the differentiating note. It should be recalled, first, that in the United States, as in England, machine industry often grew up in towns especially created for the purpose rather than in places already established. The need for water power to operate machines helped account for this, of course, but one should not overlook the awareness of the dangers of increasing the size of already existing cities, as shown by such industrial pioneers as Nathan Appleton, who helped organize textile mills, and who set up the company towns of Lowell and Waltham, Massachusetts.

Nevertheless, the small cities, new and old, grew, and their problems grew even faster than they did. Slums spread, crime and rates of crime rose. The cost of maintaining paupers troubled the taxpayers. The presence of poverty troubled tender consciences among the prosperous.

Awareness and concern produced few concrete results, however. Even men of delicate conscience were ready to let present problems solve themselves while they concentrated on the future. All would be well, many of these people reckoned, if men were properly educated. Free public schools had made New England rich and morally superior; therefore, improve existing schools and spread free education through the rest of the country.

On this score, organized workers agreed with middle-class philanthropists. Indeed, it may be argued that the latter gave respectability to what the late 1820's and early 1830's considered an essentially subversive idea: that education should be accessible to all. In the mid-twentieth century, saturated with the belief that a modern industrial society can operate only if its people achieve some degree of literacy, it seems strange to think of a time when even rudimentary literacy was regarded as a perilous accomplishment for any but the reasonably prosperous. Many Europeans regarded the United States as a threat to their way of life, and widespread ability to read counted as one factor in that threat. For people who could read would be aware of social inequity, and awareness might spur them to action. Americans, however, and especially skilled craftsmen in the seaboard towns, were coming to resent having so high a price put on learning that they could not afford it for their children without making sacrifices. They demanded that elementary education be free, tax-supported, and secular, a recognized right of all.

Rather quickly, middle-class taxpayers who had resented being asked to bear the cost of educating other men's offspring came to see how such training could be turned to their own advantage. Several decades later, in the 1880's, Henry Lee Higginson, a wealthy Bostonian who had been young in the 1840's, asked a friend to give Harvard $100,-000. His friend could afford it, said Higginson, and it was a social necessity; the United States was committed to democracy. Higginson hoped that democracy would do better for humanity than had the kings and nobles that had preceded. "Educate, and save ourselves and our families, and our money from mobs." [4] Then, too, free public schools soon came to be regarded as instruments by which the culture, as we should say, could absorb the increasing number of newcomers from Ireland, the Germanies, and England. By the early 1830's, when industry had taken hold in the North and West, crop failure and famine in Europe

[4] Bliss Perry, *Life and Letters of Henry Lee Higginson* (Boston: Houghton Mifflin, 1921), p. 329.

brought thousands of immigrants to the United States. Some were able to buy land. Many others had to stay in the seaboard towns. They were the men who dug, the strong hands and backs needed for what machinery could not yet do. Their work created wealth. Their presence intensified problems. Some of those problems are obvious: competition in the labor market, pressure on wages, crowding and its attendant filth-bred diseases. Other problems were more subtle. It is in the 1830's that we first encounter the older Americans' fear that their way of life was going to be submerged by the culture of the newcomers, that the holy Sabbath, for example, would degenerate into the Continental Sunday, when people followed churchgoing by diversion. Few native Americans of the middle class saw much relationship between the refinements of the Old World, which they admired, and the European immigrants who, more and more, became America's hewers of wood and drawers of water. The immigrant's labor was needed but he could be expected to contribute to American life only if he gave up his own identity and became "assimilated" (a word more frequently used after the 1880's, of course). In the meantime, he was accepted for his labor's sake, but usually, and particularly in cities, anxiety colored that acceptance.

As an increasingly complex economy needed and attracted a new kind of working force, so it gave rise to new groups of the dispossessed and thus generated alienation more like the modern kind than the isolation experienced by some colonial intellectuals. The newly alienated fall into three categories: the traditional artisan; the artist (and alien in all nineteenth-century industrial society); and the intellectual, often the educated son of an established family, whose place in the esteem of the community was being taken by men more successful in making money.

Skilled workmen, printers, shoemakers, tailors, and the like, resented the new economic organization which, in effect, destroyed the path to the traditional kind of advancement for artisans. Growing population in a growing nation, served by an increasing network of roads and canals, created an ever-expanding market, and this market, as John Commons pointed out many years ago, fostered a kind of mass production in inexpensive goods which antedates machine industry. This kind of large-scale production depended upon command of credit. With credit, an entrepreneur could acquire a large stock of raw material—cloth, say—pay skilled men to cut it into garments, and give out the bundled pieces to be sewn by women at home. This form of production often drove the independent craftsman out of business. By the late 1820's and the 1830's, the young skilled artisan could rarely if ever save enough from his journeyman's wages to finance him in becoming an independent producer.

The artisan was not alone in his alienation. The ferment of the 1840's expressed itself especially in the attack on slavery, the peculiar differentiating institution of the South.

During the decades before the middle 1850's, the ruling group in the North, businessmen and lawyers and politicians, Whig and Democratic, stood firm for the rights of property and did not oppose slavery. Indeed, currently, historians are discovering that a number of leaders in the anti-slavery movement can be counted among the downward mobile, people losing standing and so becoming alienated from a world where industry was establishing itself and new wealth outstripping old. Resentment at their own downward mobility sharpened their sensitivity to abuses, it is contended, and so accounts for their opinions.[5] Certainly, more anti-slavery, anti-drink, and even anti-monopoly leaders (people concerned with complicated problems of credit and currency, with which this book cannot deal) came from merchants and ministers' families than from among the increasingly wealthy factory owners.

Characteristically, many reformers tended to see social abuses as individual misdoing writ large, although, in the case of slavery, they were forced to recognize the need to change institutions. Nevertheless, some anti-slavery spokesmen showed a high level of selective inattention; the wrongs of the slaves on the Southern plantation were far more visible to their concern than the situation of child workers in Northern factories.[6] They were often quicker to advise workmen to give up whiskey and tobacco than to second union efforts to maintain wages or to replace the traditional workday—sunup to sundown—with a standard ten-hour day. Except for people like Theodore Parker—who shocked his Boston congregation by saying "thou art the man" to the distiller and the tenement-house owner as well as to the drunkard and shiftless pauper—and that curious maverick, Orestes Brownson,[7] the well-known reformers of the 1840's

[5] It is interesting that contemporary historians should focus critically on the motivation of the reformer rather than on the presence of the abuse he attacked or the relevance of the remedy he suggested.

[6] In both England and America, workingmen were quick to see the inconsistency. One of the pieces which was most frequently reprinted in the labor press is a set of lachrymose verses describing a little girl factory worker dying of overwork while the millionaire's wife and daughters ride by her home on their way to a meeting deploring the sad lot of the slave.

[7] Brownson is best known, perhaps, as the man who boxed the religious compass from strict Calvinism to Catholicism by way of Universalism, Unitarianism, and Atheism. He was a supporter of trade unions, too, and the man who brought the word "proletarian" into the English language.

showed minimal concern with the immediate problems of the urban world around them. The tenement and the pauper they tended to leave to the home mission societies and to organizations like the Association for Improving the Condition of the Poor.

Home missions began early in the nineteenth century, when churches on the Eastern seaboard became concerned lest the Western frontier lose its religious ties, lapse into illiteracy, and being illiterate, become un-Christian. Their missionaries moved westward, often preaching the Gospel with the revivalist fervor described when we discussed the Great Awakening of the middle eighteenth century. The frontier was evangelized as a result.

In a few decades it became evident that the growing cities, too, had people whose spiritual needs were being neglected. But when home missionaries brought their tracts and Bibles to the slums, they discovered that poverty tended to close ears to the message of religion. Accordingly, home mission workers began to concern themselves with alms-giving. Then, to make certain that alms did not go to the undeserving, the charitable established organizations like the Association for Improving the Condition of the Poor. Association "visitors" checked to make certain that the generous were not exploited, that people did not get money from more than one source of alms; they inspected the households of the poor for evidence of thriftless or immoral behavior—indulgence in drink particularly.

Soon this new, that is, more carefully organized, philanthropy turned to fostering self-help. Sometimes it sought a cure for poverty by urging the poor to leave the cities for the land where, it was assumed, no deserving family could fail to prosper. Generally, organized philanthropy seemed

committed to encouraging industry by making the lot of
the dependent poor as disagreeable as possible. Even kindly
people accepted this attitude because they believed that
everywhere except in the South the way had been opened
for effort to be rewarded. Only the thriftless and idle could
be really poor.[8]

By the 1840's, the cult of effort had permeated every
area of man's concern. Even in the South, the principle of
hierarchy was tending to give way. Hamilton was dead and
the heirs of his economic program had learned to shout the
slogans of equality. Jefferson and Madison, too, were dead
and their principles superseded. They had wanted opportunity for talent and virtue in life and for principle in
politics. Their successors were virtuosos of a new politics
based on bargaining among groups[9] rather than on real
clash of principle. Of course, certain questions of political
policy did arise during the 1830's and 1840's and were settled, although frequently by accident. The most important
among these issues was the attempt to restore the national
bank.

When the Second Bank of the United States was established in 1816, its charter ran for only twenty years. When

[8] Actually, it may be contended that an expanding economy in a
capital-poor country depends on a rate of profit high enough to promote investment and therefore requires low wages. Certainly, it is true
that wages in the 1840's, however favorably they might compare with
those in Europe, were not generally high enough to allow the average
industrious workman to save enough to keep his family above the
poverty line when illness or unemployment struck.

[9] To be sure, Jefferson himself had been a master in securing cooperation from disparate groups under a single political banner. His "We are
all Republicans, we are all Federalists" may have been one of the first
statements of what contemporary scholars call the *politics of consensus*.
But Jefferson knew that real differences of political philosophy did
separate him and his opponents. Any permanent organized political
grouping with no corresponding difference of principle was what was
then called "factional," and "faction" existed only to be deplored.

the Bank applied for recharter in 1832, four years before its charter actually expired, the application for renewal became a source of dispute. The struggle over rechartering the Bank continued until the charter lapsed in 1836. The institution carried on business under a Pennsylvania charter but never regained its former position. (Indeed, it ultimately failed in 1841, going down in the ruin of its president, Nicholas Biddle.) In 1840, Van Buren, who was notoriously anti-Bank, met defeat at the hands of General Harrison—a thoroughly non-political figure—sponsored by the Whigs who accepted Hamilton's ideas and intended to restore the Bank. But chance stepped in. Harrison died not many months after his inauguration and Vice-President John Tyler, who was as hostile to a national bank as any Jacksonian Democrat, succeeded him.[10]

The new orientation in politics changed political manners. Voters all but forgot the maxim that the office should seek the man. Now men chased after office and political leaders showed their quality by skill in maintaining political machines. Politics had become a business; office-seeking entered the orbit of the cult of effort.

In religious life before the Civil War, the basic paradox continued to be evident; only some men were destined to be saved, yet all men must seek salvation. But religion had long since ceased to be the primary factor in American life. Yet the element of contradiction which the old Puritan creed embodied continued to affect the national intellectual fabric. For it would seem that contradictions in theory in

[10] The Whig strategists, refusing to commit themselves to any program, had carefully balanced their non-political general with a Southern anti-Jackson man who, they reckoned, would be a merely ornamental element in the new administration. But John Tyler not only became President, but proved as unmanageable as Old Hickory himself.

one area, engendering unclear thinking, would in turn engender contradictions in other areas. Outstandingly, we find a parallel here—and the possible "spread" of a neurotic lack of logic—in the American attitude toward human liberty. Politically, the United States had asserted its principles in a statement which declared liberty to be an inalienable right of man. Yet the United States continued to permit the most obvious denial of liberty: slavery was legal in the Southern states. And with slavery, the classical conservative position held stronger ground in the South than in the North, where the road had been fully opened to effort and where, with body and with soul, however paradoxical the demand, men were expected to act to save themselves.

Yet even in the South, classical conservatism was modified. For classical conservatism requires a man to know his place and to fill it properly, not to try to get into a better place. The Southern economy produced staples for export, with slaves as its determinative labor force. In such an economy we might expect industry to lack incentive. We would expect this to be true not only for slave workers but also for the lowest level of the non-slave population. The "white trash" whose skin color was their only fortune may in some degree have written off effort as irrelevant to their situation; the slaves, of course, actually did so. But even among the "white trash" acquiescence was not entirely the rule. For Southern society before the Civil War was rather more complex than is usually recognized, and Southern culture was far more responsive to middle-class ideals than some of our twentieth-century partisans of tradition want to admit.

The great planters did indeed set the tone for the community, but that tone was not one of indifference to money. Foreign observers found that the dollar dominated men's conversation south of Washington as well as north. Raising cotton and tobacco involved men in a risky undertaking and one very definitely oriented toward money returns. Land speculation, too, was important in the South. Planter and speculator alike had money-making as a prime concern. And to a contemporary observer like James Fenimore Cooper, it was concentration on making money that made the man of business a lower creature than the aristocrat. More relevant to the line of thought we are pursuing here— concentration on speculative agriculture and speculation in land did not operate to suppress emphasis on climbing the economic ladder by hard work.[11] If one were born in a place where the ladder to economic advancement was too crowded, there were other places, and emptier, where land could be had cheaply. The West had its southern as well as its northern frontier. In books like Joseph Baldwin's *Flush Times in Alabama and Mississippi*, the likeness between the rush for gold and the rush for profit from trading in land is brought out very strikingly. Albert Pike's dialect poems illustrate another phase of the scramble for wealth on the southern frontier. Pike, himself a Connecticut man, had turned southward as other New Englanders moved west. Arkansas rewarded his endeavors and Pike cherished his new home. His verse portrait of the ambitious overseer looking toward the day when he, too, should be a rich planter from "way down yonder in Arkansas right near the Chocktaw line" is an interesting precursor of things to

[11] Indeed, in *Ishmael or From the Depths*, Mrs. E. D. E. N. South-worth, a Maryland lady, created the prototype of all the Alger heroes, and before the Civil War.

come, for it naïvely presents the vulgarity of the *nouveaux riches*, a recurrent theme in the genteel novel, at the same time that it shows the vulnerability of the innocent who is exploited by the purveyors of sophisticated urban pleasure.

Economically aspiring, money-oriented, and striving as so much of Southern society actually was, its spokesmen pictured it otherwise, the more so as sectional conflict sharpened.

In considerable degree, the conflict can be traced to the irritated awareness with which a politically skillful group— the Southerners who held a dominant position in the Democratic party—saw itself as a minority of gentlemen financially exploited by a conspiracy of merchants, bankers, shipowners, brokers, and other hangers-on. The stakes of sectional conflict may well have been control of the new land which the United States was acquiring at its neighbor's expense. But Southern spokesmen looked at the situation in a different light. People like George Fitzhugh argued that the Southern social world was to be preferred to that of the North precisely because the existence of slavery made ambitious striving a less universal imperative.

Fitzhugh and other defenders of slavery used the reports of the Parliamentary inquiries which preceded the British Factory Acts of the 1840's as a source of ammunition against an industrial society employing the labor of free men. The British worker, argued William Drayton of South Carolina (in a poem whose heroic couplets show aesthetic conservatism as well as political defensiveness), worked longer hours than the slave and for a smaller real reward: the free worker, Drayton said, ate no more; his housing was no better, and besides, he might often be unemployed. Furthermore, said Drayton, the free laborer was subject to peculiar moral hazard: he aspired to material goods and social status which he could not acquire and therefore was open to appeals from demagogues who would give him leave to prey upon his betters. In the United States, further-more, the free laborer was expected to make an effort to rise in the world, and when he failed, as he was likely to do, he would suffer psychologically as the protected slave could not.

Southern conservatives attacked the cult of effort rather indirectly nevertheless; their defense of the hierarchical principle was blunted by the need to get votes from com-mon men. Southern spokesmen scorned money-grubbing Yankees but their own involvement in a speculative econ-omy made them almost equally the slaves of money, and made their scorn sound rather paradoxical.

Before we turn to the alienated artist in the 1830's—Poe is a pattern example—we should repeat what has been said earlier: a country preoccupied with securing its subsistence and existence felt small need for the arts.[12] This barren soil was made more barren still, perhaps, by the growth of industrialism (although the agricultural South offered the artist no warmer welcome). As a result, the artist, in nine-teenth-century Europe as in the United States, often repudi-ated a world which gave him so little esteem. Yet, ironically again, this repudiation, implicit though it might be, occurred just about the time when it became possible for Americans

[12] There was some real desire for cultural independence, to be sure. Jefferson tried to have his country declare itself independent in the arts as in politics; for example, he drew the plan of a column using the cornstalk in a stylized form so that the American architect need not continue to be dependent on the acanthus of the Corinthian order. Jeffer-son was more successful as a transmitter than as an innovator in this field; he did much to bring Greek revival architecture into fashion in America, but few if any of its columns were modeled after cornstalks.

to earn a living by writing poetry and fiction. (Earning a living as painter or sculptor was a far more difficult undertaking.)

The Revolutionary generation had produced extraordinary prose, but the men who produced it did not earn their bread by writing. Nor did the younger men, including the group called the "Hartford wits," which did try to give their nation a literature in the late 1700's, and early nineteenth century, but produced only verbose epics and unsuccessful magazines. If any of this group is now in any way familiar, it is Joel Barlow, and he is remembered, when he is recalled at all, for verses in praise of Hasty Pudding.

Irving and Cooper were more successful contributors to the enterprise of giving the United States a literature of its own. Later still came the monthly magazines which published and paid for the work of American writers instead of printing and not paying English and Continental authors. (There was no international copyright.) The magazine audience was newly literate, in large part, and often composed largely of women, unsophisticated and generally committed to the morality of usefulness. A writer like Poe, dependent for his living on such an audience, was all but designed for alienation from it and from the world it represented. Poe's stories, of course, express his dislike of contemporary culture by retreat from it. Most of them take place at a time unknown to history, in a land which can be found on no earthly map. Consistently, he deals with no contemporary problems (except the murder of Mary Cecilia Rogers), and Auguste Dupin, the one character Poe did create as a person, lives in a room from which he shuts out the light of day.

Poe might have attempted to educate his audience's taste,

of course, but Poe's two potboilers, one on landscape gardening, the other on interior decoration—to be found only in his collected works—were of small use to the women who read them. They describe a luxury unobtainable by the reader of the 1830's and, to our twentieth-century taste, rather ludicrous. More typical of Poe's work was his criticism; he finds fault with Longfellow's prosody, with Lowell's "unpolished" satire, with Emerson's transcendental mistiness, and generally lashes the pretensions of ". . . that magnanimous cabal which has so long controlled the destinies of American Letters in conducting the thing called *The North American Review*." The cabal (the Establishment, we should say) struck back, punishing even the dead artist with calumny.

In the 1840's and 1850's some contemporary American writers of the North were describing industrial society with as much revulsion as Southerners like Drayton. Few twentieth-century descriptions of factories so bitterly and beautifully show man existing in despairing symbiosis with the machine as does Melville's "Tartarus of Maids." *Pierre* reeks of cold poverty in New York. In *Redburn* Melville shows mother and child starving to death in a Liverpool cellar while people walk indifferently over its grated roof. And in *Mardi* Melville presents no more flattering a portrait of his country and its institutions than James Fenimore Cooper does in that curious book called *The Monikins*.

We do not usually think of Cooper as a social critic. The Leatherstocking tales are classed as reading for children nowadays, and generally regarded as written with too much detail for the contemporary child to tolerate. Few of us know that Cooper wrote the Leatherstocking saga last chapter first, as it were: he described the destruction of proud Indians and the wilderness by that gross and sharp-witted tribe, the Chainbearers, Aaron and his sons—fit ancestors for Faulkner's Snopeses—long before he showed Chingachgook, and Uncas and Leatherstocking himself, the noble primitives whose presence said shame to modern civilized man. Like other expatriate American writers (and long residence abroad made Cooper one of the earliest of these), Cooper pined for the country from which he absented himself and found it all but intolerable when he returned. In *Home as Found* [13] he describes his countrymen in their constant assault on privacy, their contempt for good manners, their concentration on money, with all the distaste of a traveling British aristocrat. Unlike those who found Boston genteel and New York society tolerable, Cooper held no brief for the American aspirant to aristocracy. He advises visitors to Leaplow (his name for the United States in *The Monikins*) to praise the scenery and attack the people. For in Leaplow, ". . . affluence, without hesitation, or indeed, opposition, appropriated to themselves the sole use of the word respectable, while taste, judgment, honesty and wisdom, dropped like so many heir-looms [sic] quietly into the possession of those who had money." [14]

Cooper can be taken as an exponent of the eighteenth-century Jeffersonian vision of man and society who is sadly disappointed by what men in American society have made

[13] It is interesting to note that in the first half of the nineteenth century, the novel of manners in America was generally written by women, badly, for children. It is as though, by and large, no major American writer regarded the novel of manners as worth writing; perhaps he may not have taken his society seriously or he may have seen that society as too simple, or too large, for handling in a book he was capable of writing.

[14] James Fenimore Cooper, *The Monikins* (New York: G. P. Putnam Sons, 1839), p. 365.

of that vision. He may be seen as alienated, but Cooper's alienation rested rather comfortably on a landed estate: he could retire to the country and a family that provided sufficient society to keep contact with a distasteful world at a minimum.

Melville's alienation was based on harder experience and plumbed a greater depth. In *Mardi*, that strange allegorical journey through a world part fantasy and part satire, he portrays the United States as false to principles which were dubious at best. In the *Confidence Man* Melville lays the ax to the basic premise of the essential goodness of man as he both tests men's pretensions to benevolence and explores the risks of trust.

Melville wrote darkly, and when he stopped exalting the primitive in Polynesian dress, he won few readers. Emerson did not have too many readers either, but he was heard if not heeded. For Emerson earned his living by lecturing, and in his lectures he rang the changes on the theme of self-reliance.

Emerson's most notable ancestor, perhaps, was Peter Bulkeley, one of the great Puritan preachers, expounder of the logic of hellfire. Many generations later, Emerson, born into the placid fold of the successful Unitarian revolt from Calvinism, left his heritage to forge a set of orienting attitudes of his own. The Unitarian revolt began in the pre-Revolutionary period and came to maturity at the turn of the eighteenth century. At first, American Unitarianism was theologically occupied with the problem of the unity of God. Its approach to existence, logical and argumentative in method, seemed repulsively arid to many men of Emerson's generation, but it was Emerson who was most emphatic in his rejection of what he saw as mere intellectual formalism rather than a true confrontation of the universe by a self-reliant man.

Emerson left his pulpit in 1832, when he felt obliged to tell his Unitarian congregation that he could no longer administer the communion. Here one remembers Jonathan Edwards [15] announcing a change in his approach to doctrine. The two messages seem to typify the movement of New England intellectual leadership from an attempt to return to traditional Calvinism to a refusal to accept any tradition as a sufficient rock. For Edwards, true religion required a respect for the majesty of God great enough to accept, if not welcome, one's own damnation. For Emerson, true religion required a respect for the majesty of the human soul too great to allow it to depend on any inherited mode of belief or any customary form of observance. Emerson demanded that each man, searching his own soul, find in it the evidence of God's intent for him and for the universe.

The two views have in common the insistence that each man, for himself, accept responsibility for deciding whether he would claim conviction that he was saved. They part, of course, on the issue of where and how conviction was to be had. For Edwards, as we have seen, conviction was linked to God's free grace. For Emerson, conviction could come only from within a man, standing alone, in strong self-awareness. Both called on men to live in the company of loneliness, but the loneliness they contemplated did not involve the modern sense of separation from self.

[15] It will be remembered that Jonathan Edwards refused to administer the sacrament to those who did not feel able to make a full statement of conviction that they had been saved. Edwards moved back toward rigor after a long period during which a God-fearing life and adequate scriptural knowledge had been considered sufficient for admission to the communion table.

All Emerson's thinking presupposed an existent and known self. Upon this, and upon this only, man could rely. The self need not be separated from tradition, as some twentieth-century versons of romanticism seem to require; but the Emersonian self was not to be tradition's slave. Be part of your community, but be independent: have faith in your own judgment, in your own vision of the world. In varying terms, Emerson gave this message to the scholar, to the writer, and to the man in the street.

During the period after the Civil War, Emerson's message was often vulgarized into a declaration of a permanent open season for selfishness. That, of course, was scarcely Emerson's intent. He saw the growth of industrialism with a combination of admiration and dislike. The inventiveness and enterprise which characterized industrial growth gave notable testimony to the potentialities of men acting independently. But Emerson was made anxious by the way in which industrialism forced men to live out of contact with that Nature which he thought of as a source from which human wisdom and goodness drew their vitality. Emerson's Nature bore rather little relationship to the natural world which Thoreau observed with such minute leisureliness of affection. Still less does Emerson's Nature seem related to that of the exponents of the new version of natural law based on Darwinian evolution—that grim schoolmistress who keeps discipline by necessity's flogging. As we shall see in the next chapter, those who taught evolution rather than the rights of man did try to avoid the pathetic fallacy of personifying Nature. Yet reading the social Darwinists gives one the vision of a mother whose breast yields milk only to the child who bites.

Emerson's Nature was more kindly. In Nature, in the

basic structure of the universe, man could find support for the values he cherished.

If we look at Emerson in the role of lay preacher addressing the laity on behalf of those values, we see him confronting loneliness and anxiety and concerned with alienation. Emerson urges the scholar—we should say the intellectual—to keep in wholesome contact with his world, to respect the farmer, the artisan, the man of business, but he must not take that practical world for his authority any more than he had liberty to fall slackly into the arms of tradition. Like all men, the intellectual had the duty of relying upon himself, of making the effort to know that self, to accept its counsels, to fulfill the obligation of recognizing pretense and of knowing that "a popgun is a popgun though the ancient and honorable of the earth say it is the crack of doom."

The Emersonian ideal of self-reliance epitomizes the philosophy of effort before that became vulgarized in the decades after the Civil War. Yet the ideal had the seeds of vulgarization within it. Nowhere, to be sure, does Emerson approach the notion that dog-eat-dog competition is man's best road to achieving his humanity. But nowhere is there any striking awareness of man's link to his fellows. Everywhere, implicitly, is the assertion that what happens to a man is entirely his own doing. He can look to no one but himself. The community had but a tenuous existence in the Emersonian scheme; each man stood alone.

In far cruder fashion, many Americans accepted Emerson's position: effort was man's duty and effort would be, as well as bring, its own reward. Meanwhile, on every level —political, economic, social, religious—the road had been opened to effort. All adult white male citizens could generally vote and hold office by the 1850's. With the abandonment of the attempt to maintain a national bank and with the growing practice of allowing anyone who abided by certain formal and laxly enforced rules to set up a corporation, governmental checks on economic activity were all but cast aside. Legal privileges for particular religious groups disappeared, and those groups grew fastest which laid greatest stress on man's ability to attain salvation by seeking a necessary grace, which was wholly in God's power, and by leading lives rigorously directed toward achieving material success. Social barriers were beginning to fall; some diehards continued to value old family above new money, but an old family that lost its old money often discovered that suddenly old associates found its family tree faded to illegibility. Even in the South, as has been shown, flowers turned to the sun which was money. Clinging to slavery as its socio-economic base and threatened by the increasing wealth of a society based on wage labor, the South's leadership chose to secede before history should seal its minority position forever. The ensuing war, as we all know, gave legal freedom to the slave. More important, by removing the last focus of countervailing social pressure, the Civil War opened the way to the apotheosis of effort.

The Apotheosis of Effort 6

In this chapter, we discuss the basic paradox of effort as its secular form became increasingly individualistic. Before we deal with that theme, however, it seems necessary to consider the removal of that focus of countervailing pressure to which we referred at the end of the last chapter.

Common sense and good will, some historians argue, might have prevented the outbreak of the Civil War. Good will and common sense could prevent all wars; the historian's problem is discovering the factors in a situation which make men unable to use common sense and unwilling to show good will. Here, it is not relevant to explore the reasons for Americans' failure to employ sound sense after November, 1860. For our purpose, it is sufficient to remember that, on one level, the Civil War was decisive: it determined that the United States would mature as a society in which no effective social force ran counter to economic dynamism—that is, dedication to making money through the exploitation of natural resources, the financing of transportation, and the production of industrial goods. Such dedication meant that the man who acquired the largest fortune—especially if he rose from poverty—would be regarded as the worthiest human being. Soldier, poet, scholar, saint, statesman, even the gentleman himself—every figure traditionally admired—became insignificant alongside the self-made millionaire.

As we have seen, the antebellum South was far more middleclass and money-oriented than current mythmakers would have us believe. But mythology cannot arise without some base. The pre-Civil War South, committed as it was to producing agricultural staples for export, was dependent on dynamic economies in the North and in Europe, but the region's economy was not itself dynamic. It might grow, but increase in size did not mean movement toward complexity. More and more land might be brought into cotton production, for example; more and more cotton might be grown and shipped; but the producer continued to be tied to markets he did not govern and to depend on financing he did not control.

From the strictly economic point of view, the planter operating on a large scale was not the most important factor in Southern agriculture: more cotton was raised on small farms than on the lands of plantation owners. Nevertheless, the great seaboard landowners gave tone to society. Their grasp on sectional political power was loosening in the 1850's, for men of the Southwest—Mississippi, Alabama, Texas, Louisiana—people who knew themselves bound to a market, had pushed the Virginians and Carolinians out of leadership at the same time that they were often outstripping the Easterners in wealth. To be sure, the ideal was to become more firmly outlined as the society it supposedly inspired became obsolete.

The Southern ideal was directed toward creating a particular style of masculine life rather than toward the making of money, although money or credit, that is, ability to get into debt, was necessary in order to maintain the traditional

manner of slovenly lordliness decried by so many observers during the decades before the Civil War. The
stereotype of the "chivalrous Southerner" and the "money-
grubbing Yankee" was as true as any other social stereotype
which takes the place of observation. The actual function
of the Southern politician (who embodied the countervailing force of which we have been speaking) was to give
leadership to the agricultural interest throughout the nation.
This was so whether the Southerner was lord of the traditional plantation or speculative exploiter of fresh, richly
fertile land. North or South, American farmers were oriented toward expansion, toward creating more of what
already existed rather than toward the basic and continuous change which, as we have seen, was the consequence of
industrial growth.

Earlier in the Republic's history, Hamilton led those who
favored hastening industrial growth while Jefferson guided
those who opposed it, arguing that an artificially speeded
economic development would corrupt American society.
After 1825, politics took many a strange turn, but those
who accepted some elements of the Jeffersonian viewpoint
generally won the elections. Their philosophy did not govern the economy which, as we have noted, grew apace, and
in the direction of industrialization.

Elections are not fought about rational issues rationally
understood, it is currently argued, but the language of
rationality is used in politics however it may be vulgarized.
And as spoken by opponents of governmental stimulation
of economic growth, that language persuaded more voters
than did its contrary. During the period between 1825 and
1850, Southerners acquired leadership of the agricultural
interest—diverse as its membership soon became—and they

succeeded in preventing Federal support of anything approaching a Hamiltonian program. After the middle 1830's, legislation to further central banking, protective tariffs, Federal assistance to railroad building, and the operation of ocean steamships was effectively blocked. The failure of such legislation is sometimes taken to mean that the American economy, before the Civil War, developed slowly.

It is assumed that Northern victory cleared the way for a burst of industrial progress. Actually, this is not entirely true. Statistics are incomplete; nothing like reliable continuous figures are available before 1869, and some of the material for the succeeding years is also inadequate. W. W. Rostow, however, has employed available information to reach the conclusion that the United States had completed what he calls *take-off* by 1860. By that year, he declares, the American economy had become sufficiently diversified to be no longer properly agricultural; it had passed into the stage of self-sustaining economic growth.[1]

The Civil War, however, did clear the way for the entrepreneur's dominance. He received all he asked in the way of governmental favors; his activities were hampered by few regulations, and his taxes were minimal. This situation prevailed, to a considerable degree, because without Southern leadership the agricultural interest proved unable and, for the time, even unwilling to oppose Federal policies which fostered industry and finance at its expense. Farmers, North and South, produced the agricultural staples whose export provided a favorable balance of trade for the nation.

[1] W. W. Rostow, *Stages of Economic Growth* (Cambridge: Cambridge University Press, 1961), p. 95; Rostow, *Process of Economic Growth* (Oxford: Oxford University Press, 1960), p. 319. Take-off was not simultaneous in all sections of the country: New England was first to experience it; it did not occur in the South until about 1930.

Because of high tariffs, they paid higher prices for the
manufactured goods they needed (it is argued by some proponents of high tariffs, they got a larger market to sell in).
And they helped repay the nation's Civil War creditors in
money more valuable (in terms of purchasing power) than
that which had been lent. But a decade passed before they
voiced complaint.

Between 1865 and 1877 the radical shift in legislative
policy which had occurred during the war was sharpened
and solidified. Southern representation was controlled—
often by manipulation of the new Negro voters as well as
by disenfranchisement of the white community's leaders
and by gerrymandering—in order to give the Republicans
majorities in Congress. In 1876, because of the depression
following the panic of 1873 and the scandals of the Grant
administration,[2] the Democrats won a majority of the popular vote. The electoral vote was almost evenly divided; the
votes of Florida, Louisiana, South Carolina, and Oregon
were in dispute.[3] It has been said that an honest count would

[2] A full discussion of these would require several volumes. Fraudulent
procurement contracts were common. The Department of Justice spent
money to influence New York City elections and the Attorney General
warned Federal district attorneys not to grant immunity to informers
reporting frauds in the payment of the tax on whiskey. Grant's private
secretary was deeply involved in these same Whiskey Ring frauds; his
brother had bought and sold post-traderships in Indian territory, then a
profitable enterprise. Grant allowed his Secretary of War to resign just
before a congressional committee could bring impeachment charges
against him for taking bribes. *See* Allan Nevins, *Abram S. Hewitt* (New
York: Harper & Brothers, 1935), pp. 291, 301.

[3] An Oregon elector had died between election and the formal electoral
count. The question rose as to his replacement. The Republicans argued
that the two Republican electors should choose a man to replace the
dead elector; the Democrats insisted that the vacant place should go to
the elector with the next highest number of votes (a Democrat). In a
close election, even a single electoral vote was important, but the dispute
really centered around the electors of the three Southern states.

have awarded the Southern votes to the Democrats, but an honest election (with no intimidation of Negro voters) would have given those votes to the Republicans.

The Compromise of 1877 awarded the contested votes to the Republican Rutherford B. Hayes and promised Southern leaders undisturbed rule of their states; at this time, the Federal government gave up all effort to protect the Negro's right to vote. That sorry story, so important in its political consequences for our own time, has but little to do with our main theme. Here we are concerned with the farmers' abandonment of the political alliance joining farmers from West and South which, before the Civil War, gave the agricultural interest so significant a role in national affairs. As we have seen, that alliance had operated, mainly under Southern leadership, to further the farmers' interests, at least by denying special privileges to industry.

The Civil War destroyed that alliance. Even after the Compromise of 1877 "liberated" the South to become solidly Democratic, it was not reconstituted. Farmers, North and South, continued to vote as emotional appeals to sectional patriotism directed. Western Republicans, particularly, recalling shared battles and wounds, waved the bloody shirt, and behind that banner farmers marched, voting Republican and supporting policies which speeded economic growth at their own cost. The Democrats in the South, too, waved the bloody shirt, and used its appeal to form the political entity known as the Solid South. To Southern voters, as to the farmers of the nation, the Democratic party did offer a program of some relevance: it advocated lower tariffs and a measure of currency inflation. But the appeal of these practical proposals was insufficient to offset the bitterness of lingering wartime emotion. And the national

Democratic party produced no charismatic leadership at this time.

Farmers complained, of course; they agitated. By the middle 1880's they organized and voted in protest. But they did not form a stable new party or even an adequately powerful force in the old parties. Not until the 1930's were farmers able to get as good a place at the trough of privilege as the industrialists had enjoyed since the Civil War.

To repeat, with the slaveholding planters removed or restricted as leaders of a ruling political group, the economic dynamism of industrialization had no counterbalance either in the political arena or among the leaders of American thought. Meanwhile, the nation matured industrially. Its railway net was built, however shoddily; its banking and currency system operated, however clumsily; its industries grew, however brutally. Methods of production took forms we recognize as modern. Mechanization increased. The assembly line appeared. Eli Whitney, we recall, invented interchangeable parts [4] and his invention had been applied in many industries. Now further rationalization of the processes of manufacture began to be practiced. Carrying Whitney's invention forward, American wagon makers put wagon bodies on waist-high moving belts for workmen to attach wheels and axles.

Governmental assistance to entrepreneurial effort produced results. Continued real economic development accompanied the startling growth of individual fortunes. By 1890 the United States was producing a large proportion of the world's industrial raw materials—coal, oil, copper, iron —and a great part of its food and fiber as well. American steel output, a key measure of industrialization, outstripped

[4] *See* p. 104.

Britain's. In the forty years between 1850 and 1890, the national wealth rose from $8.43 billion to $65 billion (in figures not corrected for changes in purchasing power). The costs of growth were high to be sure, but those costs were largely borne by people who did not count. Millhands and miners were imported by the shipload, paid what the market could bear, thrown onto their own resources when trade fell off or they were injured in accidents. Farmers were helpless to deal with falling prices for their products. Mine owners were better able to combine and protect themselves against market fluctuations. Business geniuses like the elder Rockefeller developed ways of eliminating wasteful competition—and their competitors. Money moved into the pockets of those best able to make more money with it.

By the middle 1880's the depression which had begun with the great panic of 1873 had tapered off. And the economy's growth had transformed making money into the proper business of man. Except for a few writers—Henry George in *Progress and Poverty* and Henry Demarest Lloyd in *Wealth Against Commonwealth* being perhaps the best remembered—the leaders of thought and the makers of public opinion burned incense on the altar of successful effort. For effort had wrought more than wonders of production. It was responsible for what was said to be the nineteenth century's visible moral superiority to its predecessors. As a link between people, the relationship of employer and wage earner was considered more respectable than the bonds of custom and allegiance—both rigid and personal—which once had been the formal tie between men. The exchange of money, it was claimed, represented no subservience. Nevertheless, in fact, the old leaven lingered sourly. Long after employers had dropped even the vocabulary of human concern for those they hired, the employee was expected to be grateful for being hired. Action against an employer had a color of moral error, especially if such action were taken jointly with other workers.

Evidence that old attitudes persisted did not much concern social theorists in the era between 1870 and 1890. Among intellectuals outside the church—and they were increasing in number—evolution through natural selection had, as Richard Hofstadter points out,[5] become more than a way of understanding biological fact; it was a normative principle, the creed of a secular faith whose core was the moral value of struggle in the economic arena. For out of struggle, by each, against all, in a market place controlled by none, had come the social increment which the nineteenth-century world was so efficiently enjoying.

Yet, according to this theory, the effort which was so fruitful produced its benefits only within a context of overarching process. Man's struggle and his self-direction did create all social good, but only as a by-product. Any considered effort to achieve social good—to mitigate the impact of depressions, for example—would necessarily be self-defeating, whether measures were taken by government or by groups of men acting together, because public action to blunt the thrust of market forces, if it succeeded, would operate to diminish individual industry. Less wealth would be produced accordingly, and society as a whole would be, if not positively impoverished, at least less rich. Private joint action to protect men against the operation of the market would have no better result than, say, the British poor law

[5] Richard Hofstadter, *Social Darwinism in America* (New York: George Braziller, 1959).

of 1795.[6] (Even carefully safeguarded almsgiving encouraged pauperism.) Since wages were set by natural law —the ratio between the number of workers, the number of jobs in the economy, and the amount of capital available for wage payments—trade union action to maintain or to raise wage levels could not succeed. Union influence, it was claimed, did force the industrious workman to hold down his output and did burden the employer with unnecessarily high costs. Fewer enterprises would be started; accordingly, fewer jobs would be open, and actually wages would fall.

Yet the goal of decent lives for all men, these theorists [7] said, had not been abandoned: the laws of society worked obliquely; self-interest led to the good of all—if only each man would continue to be constructively selfish.

With the migration to the United States of the 1880's and the 1890's—a westward flow which should rank with the great historic movements of people—there came an obvious and increasing alienation of master from man and worker from worker. Large-scale immigration was not new; immigrants had swelled the American working force since the 1830's. Now, however, the movement was spurred and intensified. Railroads with land to sell, steamship companies with holds to fill, contractors needing work gangs to dig the sewers and lay the gas mains and trolley tracks for growing cities—all sent agents into the peasant lands of

[6] This had finally provided that agricultural laborers who could not support their families on their wages should receive supplementary relief from taxes. The law held wages down, but taxes rose. More damaging, according to the views summarized here, the law encouraged people to stay and breed in rural areas instead of moving to towns where, if they did not prosper, few of their children would live to trouble the taxpayer.

[7] One of the strongest proponents of this point of view was William Graham Sumner, author of "What Social Classes Owe to Each Other" and, more familiar nowadays, *Folkways*.

Italy and Austria-Hungary as well as into Scandinavia and Germany. Fulfilling the anticipations of Henry Carey, one of America's pioneers in economic theory, ships carried American materials abroad and brought back more valuable cargo—men. For three decades at least, until the outbreak of World War I, the American economy got a large part of its labor supply free: young men were imported ready-made, their unproductive childhoods paid for by the societies in which they were born.

These young men (and women too, although the new immigration had a male surplus) were, in large part, Roman Catholics and spoke either the dialects of the illiterate or unfashionable languages like Polish and Croatian. Speech and religion alike set these workers apart from their supervisors and employers. And the employer was an increasingly distant figure as enterprises grew larger and more complex. More and more plants were owned by large corporations; more and more corporations were managed by men who had no real contact with the production worker: the man who sweated in the steel mill; the woman who stitched shoes at the machine. Foremen and supervisors, working in the same shop, were frequently of different origin than their crews. Religion might have operated as a bond between people working together, but language was divisive. Men from the same homeland tended to clump together, and for many the real homeland was an isolated region considered remote and barbarous even in its own metropolis. In the huddlings of immigrants, alienation was often more evident than fraternity, for those most skillful in adapting to new ways of living exploited the less flexible.

Adding to this alienation another factor arose: increasingly, work became ever more impersonal.[8] The worker was becoming an interchangeable part. Mechanization intensified the alienating effect of producing for the market, and the speed which mechanization exacted added to the impoverishment of the person. To twentieth-century eyes, the factory hand in the 1880's might move slowly, but in comparison to the pace of work on the land—except at harvest—the speed-up had begun in mill, factory, and mine, and had added a new dimension to the curse of labor.

In our own world, we are becoming increasingly aware of how greatly we and our culture have been and are impaired by the gulf between the worker and his work, by the widespread feeling (often obscure to the person himself) that the task by which a man earns his paycheck is without meaning, without essential relation to his self.

Each improvement in transportation in the United States meant an expanded market, and each widening of the market gave further advantage to the man with a flair for finance, and disadvantaged the craftsman who hoped to market the goods he himself made—perhaps with the assistance of a small working force. During the 1820's and 1830's, when the impact of this change was most acutely felt by American artisans, spokesmen for early trade unions voiced their resentment of the situation and their desire for a return to an older relationship to work. After the panic of 1837, American trade unions went into a long period of decline; when they revived, just before the Civil War, many unions tended to become more realistic, that is, to concen-

[8] This situation was hailed enthusiastically by a self-conscious representative of his class, steel magnate Andrew Carnegie who rejoiced that "... In the place of the skilled workman there is a machine tender whose duty is simply to watch the machine and see that it does its work properly." *Triumphant Democracy* (New York: Charles Scribner's Sons, 1893), p. 113.

trate on the price paid for working rather than on a man's contentment with his work.

Yet not until the failure of the Knights of Labor in the middle 1880's did the major organizations of American workmen definitely, and on principle, give up concern with the larger social framework within which they struggled for their pay. Nevertheless, except in special instances—the United Mine Workers in the isolated coal towns of Pennsylvania, for example—the worker did not create out of his organizations any psychological or social sustenance which could balance the forces making for alienation. The collapse of the Knights of Labor, an organization which did have a social vision, however fuzzy, left most unions with no real political orientation, no concept of any alternative to the society in which the worker existed. In large cities, cheap amusements were already available and offered more pleasurable distraction to the tired laborer than the earnestness inseparable from union social activities. (In the company coal towns, however, the miner had few opportunities for commercial recreation.) The refuge of the church—particularly for Catholic workers who frequently found in it a familiar part of the Old Country—must not be forgotten in this context.

We have said that the so-called new immigration was disproportionately male and often only partly separated from its home. For with the multiplication of passenger steamships, it became rather common for men to leave their European homes, work in America—living miserably so that they might save—and then return with money enough to pay old debts or buy bits of land. One may conjecture that more men came with this plan in mind than were able to fulfill it and that, accordingly, families were often broken up. The wife abandoned by a husband gone off to America became part of Yiddish lore and drama, a cliché situation guaranteed to set an audience snuffling.

In families which migrated together, another kind of alienation soon became evident: parent and child were strangers. In our time, the gulf between child and parent is a deplored commonplace of psychological discussion. During the decades before the First World War, however, children of immigrants were encouraged to widen and deepen the gulf.[9] For when the worthy and worrying part of the community became aware of the new immigration, it began to fear for the integrity of the national identity. Americans, after all, were "essentially British. I trust that they are ever more to remain truly grateful for this crowning mercy," wrote Andrew Carnegie; nevertheless, he felt that there was no reason to fear serious injury to the nation from the regrettable influx of southern Europeans.[10] Others were less confident than Carnegie; they were ready to raise at least some barriers against immigration even if labor became dearer as a result. Still others had more faith in their culture; they undertook to Americanize the new immigrant.

And the easiest immigrant to attack was the child: his receptivity was heightened by those basic psychological antagonisms with which Freud has made us familiar. To be sure, the American child had long been known as an obstreperous creature. But the brashness of "Young America" in the 1840's and 1850's was something very different from the cleavage between parent and child in the immigrant

---

[9] As will be remarked later, appreciation of the contribution of the immigrant to our culture did not become fashionable in the United States until the main source of that contribution had dried up.

[10] Carnegie, *op. cit.*, p. 38.

family. "Young America" had spoken its parents' language; it lived in their economic and social world. Its refractoriness was a direct product of that world. Its quarrel with its elders was rooted in desire to control the world—and in a hurry.

The immigrant child often wanted to be out of its parents' world. Furthermore, and as disturbing, the traditional family roles were reversed in America. The immigrant parent, as Geoffrey Gorer points out, could not initiate his child into his culture. Rather it was the child who took the parent by the hand. For the child spoke English, though it might be only the English of slum streets or country schools. The child could read, an accomplishment not always common among immigrant parents. And the immigrant child was taught to aspire in every way that the woman who ruled his classroom knew how to teach aspiration.

The content of aspiration tended to be a desire to cast the skin of Old Country tradition, to lose all odor of Old Country origin, to put on an American skin. The children and grandchildren of the more successful aspirants may voyage long and far in search of roots. But many immigrants had rejected their roots long before they left their own countries; the New World called to those most likely to feel alien in the Old, to people whose home gave them nothing. Though the custodians of European society, when the great outpouring was rising to a crest, urged peasants to stay on their land and show loyalty to lord and emperor by increasing the supply of agricultural labor and bringing down its cost, the greedy wanted to eat meat more than four times a year, and the suggestible had heard that one could, in America.

Since the Old Country had refused the immigrant the

life that he sought, he was willing to see his children turn their backs on it. But when his child asserted himself on the ground of superior knowledge, the immigrant parent resisted. The child often left home then, throwing off older attachments in ways which made new continuities harder to develop.

However the child of the new immigration may have suffered, he was apt to be inarticulate. It was the descendants of an older immigration—people who had come from Europe before 1850—who developed a kind of sensitivity which expressed itself in writing. And it is the work of these older Americans that shows a facet of alienation which differentiates the artist from the rest of society in this country. That difference is related to a peculiar characteristic of American life, what may be called its "future-directed" quality. In the United States, life is always about to be so much better that its present deficiencies can be ignored. But the artist lives in a present which he must see truthfully. Often, therefore, it is the novelist or the poet who sees his world as it is, whereas the practical man (and especially if he has a stake in economic growth) sees that world in the light of its becoming, of what he hopes it will be.

E. W. Howe, the author of the *Story of a Country Town*, would have called himself a practical rather than a sensitive man. He was a successful newspaper owner and editor and, in very large degree, a disciple of the cult of self-sufficient struggle in the market place and of the notion that the hindmost who fall into the devil's hands deserve no better master. Howe thought himself a down-to-earth Kansan, even if acutely aware of his neighbors' faults. Yet in the *Story of a Country Town*, Howe helped shape the

American literary genre known as "the revolt from the village." Fairview, as Howe calls his town, is a place where no one would want to live, inhabited by people no one would want to live with. But the virtues Howe extolled in his editorials—the successful pursuit of money, thrift, prudence, and hard work—these very virtues created the unlovely world he portrays. The inhabitants of Fairview earn their living by charging farmers all the traffic will bear and giving as little as possible in return. They claim to worship a loving God by treating men without love, and reward themselves for good behavior by punishing their neighbors, devoting themselves, as Howe's latest editor shows, to mediocrity and small hates.[11]

Mark Twain wrote on another level, but he, too, was in revolt against the village, for all that he often fell into its Philistinism. *Huckleberry Finn* has been labeled a book for boys, yet the Brooklyn librarian who, in 1905,[12] wanted it taken off the shelves of the children's room shot near the mark. She objected to the story because its prose was ungrammatical and its moral dangerous: it showed idleness to be a greater virtue than industry in a boy. But *Huckleberry Finn* does more: it encourages rebelliousness against social norms; it portrays parent-figures as wicked or stupid; it makes the young guide the old (as a slave and a Negro, Jim is perpetually "boy"); above all, it portrays the common man as vulgar, mean, and cowardly.

Like the greater novel, *Puddin'head Wilson* disguises its essentially subversive character although, unlike *Huckle-*

---

[11] E. W. Howe, *Story of a Country Town*, edited by Claude M. Simpson (Cambridge, Mass.: Belknap Press of the Harvard University Press, 1961).

[12] *Mark Twain's Autobiography*, Vol. II (New York: Harper & Brothers, 1924), pp. 334-39.

berry Finn, it does not dwindle into childish nonsense. At the end of *Puddin'head Wilson*, the Southern shibboleth, "blood will tell," has been so ambiguously treated that one is certain only that mother love—the slave woman has put her own nearly white son into the white master's cradle—exists and that it has destroyed both the child it cherished and the child it deprived of a birthright. For the slave reared as master is overindulged and grows up a cowardly brute, and the master reared a slave cannot feel at home in the inheritance he has regained.

In *Puddin'head Wilson*, too, Mark Twain shows the small Southern town—bleak, smug, and hateful—twin to E. W. Howe's Fairview.

Hamlin Garland's novels appeared after the early 1880's, when Howe and *Huckleberry Finn* were first published. Garland deals with a life more completely rural than that which they depict, and his distaste for the life he presents is animated by resentment against the bankers and merchants and middlemen who exploit the farmer. Garland lets us see the exploited as exploiting; the farmer's wife and children pay for some of his frustrations. *A Daughter of the Middle Border* shows a woman's suffering. *A Son of the Middle Border* tells how a sensitive youth saw the Plains frontier as a place from which to escape. Garland not only criticized his country in his writing, as Howe and Twain did; like Mark Twain, he acted—he left his home for the East. But Boston, Garland's first objective, had lost its position. By this time, the American seeking civilization went to New York or Europe; Boston was merely refined.

Henry James left America completely although he continued to write about Americans in Europe, finding rich material in the confrontation of the two civilizations. Yet in his life, James was very American in expressing alienation: he left what he considered barren soil and sought out more fertile regions, a society of sufficiently complex social differences to supply the novelist of manners with the themes he needed.[13] Social differences did exist in post-Civil War America, but they existed only to be knocked down, not to torment the men who respected them.

In his work, although James starts with the naïve American defeated by European civilization, we see his protagonists changing places. In *The American* (1877) Christopher Newman is deprived of the woman he loves and who returns his love by the conniving of her French family. In *The Ambassadors* (1903) the American sent to rescue a young countryman from the French siren into whose hands he has fallen discovers that it is she who is being betrayed. And at last, in *The Golden Bowl* (1904) James shows equally "naïve" Americans ruthlessly taking possession of the spoils of Europe, of the art and the people they have bought. It must be said, however, that it is difficult to know whether James was aware of all that he was saying or of the criticism of his fellow countrymen that he had made. Thus, in *The Golden Bowl* James calls Maggie Verver, whose father had bought Prince Amerigo for her, "wonderful" even while he shows her manipulations enforcing her rights of ownership. Is his adjective sarcasm, one wonders, or does James truly admire the inexorable love of his heroine? Does the crack in the bowl imply that the Americans were

[13] In his notebooks and later in his life of Hawthorne, James remarked that the United States had no court, nobility, army, clergy, diplomatic service, no palaces, castles, ivied universities, village ale-houses, sport, race courses, political society, fox-hunting, country gentlemen, picturesque peasants, novels, pictures or museums. *See* F. O. Matthiessen and Kenneth B. Murdock (eds.), *The Notebooks of Henry James* (New York: George Braziller, Inc., 1955), p. 14.

buying damaged goods after all? Or are we to take the bowl which is beautiful as well as cracked as a symbol of the essentially flawed character of an existence which must be accepted on its own terms?

As James shows us how Adam Verver and his daughter made certain that they get all Verver has paid for, one becomes aware of the spirit which created the self-made millionaire. And here we approach another aspect of alienation. The later half of the nineteenth century is characterized by separation between the successful American and the political community within which he functioned. In the period after the Civil War, we observe a noteworthy departure from the development of other countries: the people who owned the United States—or rather the most modern and profitable sectors of its economy—did not become a ruling class of the conventional sort. Many spent their money and brought pressure upon their employees in order to manipulate elections, parties, and candidates and so determine legislative policy, but working through others as they generally did, they could not be held to account by the voters. The Constitution of the United States provides for representative and responsible government, but from the end of the Civil War till the early 1900's, the nation was controlled by people who refused to be visible and responsible governors.[14]

Here, the singular prose to which Andrew Carnegie put his name is worth citing: "The Republic has a reserve of pure and distinguished men to guide her councils. . . . When

[14] Currently, some historians are arguing that the very character of the system which developed in the United States after 1800 dissolved political authority and precluded effective government, particularly in the area of economic regulation. *See*, for example, Wallace D. Farnham, "The Weakened Spring of Government," *American Historical Review*, Vol. LXVIII (April, 1963), pp. 636-62.

the ship of state is in smooth waters, more important matters require its attention and the governing power goes below; yet mark you, when the wind blows, this captain walks the deck." [15]

There were those whose behavior gave Carnegie's statement the lie. Abram S. Hewitt was an important figure in the iron industry and took an active, visible part in the political life of his day—and as a Democrat at that. In the House of Representatives, he served as a member of the Foreign Affairs Committee which inquired into another of the Grant administration scandals, the Emma Mine affair.[16] He championed sound money and lower tariffs and tried to make government more efficient. In the Republican party, too, young Theodore Roosevelt showed that the "better element" did not always retreat from the roughhouse which was New York politics.

Hewitt and Roosevelt were the exceptions, however; Carnegie expressed the rule when he said, "the ablest and best men of the Republic are not found as a class trifling their time away [in politics]." Disregard of political responsibility because of the conviction that any interference with the working of natural law caused evil might have seemed acceptable in an intellectual climate ruled by the Jeffersonian conviction that government should have only the most limited sphere of activity. (Actually the men of Jefferson's generation and persuasion were zealous in their service of the limited state.) But Jefferson's humanistic

[15] Carnegie, *op. cit.*, p. 69.

[16] The American Minister to England had, Hewitt's investigation showed, been deeply and shamelessly involved, along with Senator Stewart of Nevada, in a scheme to sell stock in a Utah silver mine. In exchange for a gift of stock, the Minister publicly endorsed the mine's soundness—actually, the enterprise was vastly speculative—and when he learned that, in spite of his endorsement, the stock was falling, he tried to sell it short. *See* Allan Nevins, *op. cit.*, pp. 301-302.

orientation was very different from the hard-bitten, essentially money-centered theorizing which set Darwin on the shoulders of Adam Smith and, combining ideas drawn from the theory of natural selection with the economics of laissez-faire, created that system of asserting "whatever is, is right" which Richard Hofstadter has labeled "social Darwinism."

Among the exponents of this philosophy, William Graham Sumner ranks high. Trained for the ministry but unable to accept received doctrine, Sumner turned to what we should term the social sciences; indeed, he ultimately became one of the founders of modern American sociology. He brought into his teaching at Yale and into his writing on economics and social issues something of the fervor of a seventeenth-century New England preacher. In essays like "What Social Classes Owe to Each Other," Sumner spoke as champion of the "forgotten man," the industrious citizen who minded his business and paid his bills. This man, said Sumner, owed no other group anything but obedience to the law which they had agreed should govern all. Recognition of other kinds of obligation ultimately amounted to granting the improvident the right to exploit the provident.

Views resembling Sumner's tended to prevail in the academic world, where Herbert Spencer's influence was increasing. Those views were individualistic and exalted the economically independent man: he faced the chances of the market place unflinchingly, alone; he did not seek to evade the verdict of that tribunal by calling upon outside help.[17] In the context of such a social outlook, alienation and loneliness are good, not evil, for they bear witness to

[17] In recalling the lives of such apostles of this viewpoint as James Mill and Spencer himself, it is amusing to remember that they should have had their own work, which could not have survived in the literary market place, subsidized by friends.

independence, to freedom from personal allegiance and emancipation from bondage to inherited status. Division between man and man, between worker and employer, meant real liberty for all. The exchange of money bound men where bonds were relevant and left them unfettered in other respects. Division between man and his community also constituted liberation. A citizen obeyed the law. He cast his vote and paid his taxes, and that was the end of it. The cash nexus which Carlyle so despised was considered, in American academic circles, to be the only truly honorable link between men in their socio-economic relationships.

Bald summaries of this sort may sound like caricature. Exposure to the writings of the social Darwinists and to the unexpressed major premises of the writers of the inferior fiction of the 1870's and 1880's leaves the reader feeling that sociability and family life, necessary though they might be, were merely recreation, the means by which men were strengthened for the true focus of life, the struggle of the market place. In the nature of things, men might be defeated there, but struggle was an end in itself; out of struggle came strength for future struggle.

Theories like Sumner's reflect nineteenth-century social atomization even as they describe and justify it. Nineteenth-century social fact and the theory which grew out of it help us understand something of the peculiar texture of twentieth-century American life, and particularly the emotional shallowness which the psychotherapist sees in so many patients and which the perceptive European traveler encounters in so many of his superficially friendly hosts. The ethos of alienation, which has just been sketched, affected more than men's economic lives. People are what they do. If the main emphasis is on the impersonal pursuit of wealth, it is the rare individual who, outside his working hours, will be able to give substance to his personal relations. In these hours, too, money will be his emotional nexus.

The precepts of self-interest, of course, contradicted the Christian morality which most successful Americans professed, but the style of life which the Puritans brought with them was itself divided, affected by the paradox of the demand for effort from men whom effort could not help, so far as the salvation of their souls was concerned. Churches which held strictly to this creed had lost ground, to be sure, but the paradox still worked subterraneously. The American of the nineteenth century rarely questioned the possibility of serving both God and Mammon, for his service of Mammon *was* the service of God.

Reinforcing the cult of the self-made man, the legend of Abraham Lincoln began to take shape in both popular and scholarly writing, creating Lincoln not merely in the earlier image of the folk hero—homely, strong, shrewd jokester—but as the model of the man who had raised himself by his own bootstraps, who had moved out of obscure poverty to become President and savior of his country.[18] What Lincoln had done, and Andrew Carnegie (on another level), any American boy could do.

The cult of the self-made millionaire and even of the savior-President might be regarded with reservation by some. But in another sort of American myth—if we can call the lowest level of popular fiction mythological—the self-made man was adored without reservation. As the works of Mrs. E. D. E. N. Southworth and Horatio Alger presented that hero, he bore small relation to the self-made

[18] With a small reach of the imagination, Lincoln can be taken as an American version of that ancient religious archetype, the king who dies for his people.

man of the real world. There the successful, like Jay Gould, lied and cheated and bulldozed his way. But the hero of fiction was more than scrupulous. Mrs. Southworth's *Ishmael*, a young lawyer, would defend only innocent clients. Alger's youths scorned "tricky deals" and usually managed to get the better of those who tried to make them the victims of such "smartness." And in the land of myth, success was often dependent on winning someone's favor. The brave young bootblack stopped a runaway horse and saved the merchant's daughter. What could the merchant do but give the young man a job? For then thrift and industry won their opportunity. Merit reinforced courage and luck. Then the merchant's daughter married her rescuer and everyone lived happily ever after.

Although the role of luck in popular fiction served to dilute the gospel of effort, the importance assigned to luck may be taken as a degenerate form of "election" in the Calvinist sense.

Few readers consciously equated luck and election, to be sure, and it may seem farfetched to find formative social images in the literary bargain basement. Yet American young people were apt to read dime novels avidly, frequently finding them the more delightful because they were forbidden, and the reading of youth is influential. If even the serious novel derives from the daydream, surely successful trash wins its audience because it offers the reader unmitigated fantasy in a form which makes no demands on his intelligence.

The concept of effort in politics entailed other paradoxes than those which we have just been considering. The entrepreneur's activity, exploiting the gifts of nature and the ingenuity of man, produced enormous economic growth.

Economic growth brought a new awareness of national power and that awareness awakened a desire in the hearts of many influential Americans to have their country respected in the international arena, preferably without assuming responsibilities.

The most significant manifestation of that ambition was the Spanish-American War. Currently, historians tend to interpret that conflict as the outcome of manipulation of popular emotion for political ends rather than for economic purposes. The business community, so far as its will can be explored, seems to have been generally opposed to the war. Many political leaders, on the other hand, regarded war— especially "a splendid little war," to quote John Hay, McKinley's Secretary of State—as a means of keeping themselves in power while evading economic problems, such as the need to reorganize an unwieldy, inefficient banking and currency system, the need to reform the tariff, to make regulation of railroads more effective, and to deal with an increasing degree of concentration of economic power. Economic problems which had been ignored for decades had finally come to the surface of politics. And in 1896 William Jennings Bryan and the partisans of currency inflation through the free coinage of silver had won control of the Democratic party from the conservative faction identified with former President Grover Cleveland and the gold standard.

The defenders of things as they were saw war as a means of diverting national concern and so choking off further attempts by the farmers to avenge the defeat which they experienced in 1896. The desire for hegemony in the Western Hemisphere of course was also a factor; England and Germany might move against Spain if the United States did not. Victory in the Spanish-American War made the United States a modern imperial power as it acquired most of the empire which a declining Spain had retained.

This situation, too, had its paradoxes. The outcome of a war said to be for freedom (the freedom of Cuba from Spanish oppression) was a subsequent war of conquest, for the Philippines had to be subjugated before they could be effectively annexed. A second outcome of the war was the shrinkage of the orbit of civil liberties. In a confused series of opinions, the Supreme Court decided that some parts of the Constitution were more fundamental than others. And only those fundamental portions applied to the newly acquired territories. Apparently, the Bill of Rights could not be categorized as fundamental since, in certain instances, the right to trial by jury and the right to publish were more narrowly circumscribed in the new territories than they were in the continental United States.

Thus, a war said to be for freedom entailed the consequence of America's becoming indisputably an imperial power, with all that meant in the way of enforcing its will and its concepts of the good and proper life upon what Kipling called "the lesser breeds without the law."

Doubts and Changes 7

DURING THE DECADES after the Civil War, individual thrift and application came to be regarded as the source of all human good. As a corollary, giving people opportunity to pile up huge fortunes unrestrained by anything but bare legality was held to promote the welfare of society. Acquisitiveness prevailed, but the theory of its rectitude did not command all men's minds. We have seen how some artists expressed their alienation from the world which acquisitiveness had made. In this chapter, we go on to consider four other ways in which men expressed their uneasiness in the world which was coming into being in the United States. We shall deal with the paradox implicit in the new outburst of philanthropy, with the beginnings of government regulation of economic life, with the divided mind of trade unionism or rather with the incongruity between its pronouncements and its practices, and with the dilemma that confronted the "better element" when a number of its members finally became concerned with political reform.

The new philanthropy, organized and directed toward the establishment of institutions, can be traced to the 1830's and 1840's, when groups like the Association for Improving the Condition of the Poor were set up. After the 1870's and 1880's, when the groundwork of many of the great Ameri-

can fortunes was laid, the men who had acquired them began to spend huge sums on a great variety of philanthropic
enterprises. People who held that what could not maintain
itself in the market place had no right to exist gave money
away by the tens of millions—and that in a period when
the absence of income taxes made such gifts neither an
indirect saving nor a means of thwarting a governmental
policy of which the giver disapproved.

A number of motives animated the new philanthropy.
Like the charitable bequests of the Middle Ages, nineteenth-
and twentieth-century gifts and endowments may be interpreted as expiation of guilt. Occasionally, the giving was
said to express gratitude to the country and the institutions
which had allowed the giver to accumulate his wealth.
Later, and perhaps more rarely, individual giving seems to
be a measure of social defense, an attempt to improve the
giver's public "image," as current jargon puts it.

Whatever the motive, the paradox is evident. It is, of
course, related to the general ability of men to hold, without
too much awareness of their incongruity, divergent views
about the proper relation betweeen those who had succeeded and those who had not. In this instance, the older
ideal of stewardship was able to coexist with the ideal of
competitive acquisitiveness. Calvin himself had accepted the
concept of stewardship: those who showed themselves the
Lord's elect, giving evidence of such virtues as thrift and
prudence in their lives, would succeed and, by their success,
indicate whose favor they had enjoyed. Since success was
thus not their own doing, the prosperous had an obligation
to deal with their gains as the Lord's stewards rather than
as mere possessors.

Stewardship was not always directly synonymous with

charity and, in one sense, the ideals of stewardship and competitive acquisitiveness actually tended to reinforce each other by giving the reinvestment of profit a high moral standing. Reinvesting for further gain increased society's capital while it gave work to ever-rising numbers of the less fortunate, whereas self-indulgent consumption,[1] it was then thought, could employ only a limited number of persons.

But the Lord's steward was expected to do more than allow others to gain as an incident of making his own fortune. He was expected to share the Lord's bounty. The new philanthropy reconciled the conflict between economic principle and the Biblical assurance that he who gives to the poor lends to the Lord by directing itself toward projects which would make people better able to help themselves. Higher levels of wealth and education seemed most likely to achieve this end; hence, old colleges and universities were more richly endowed and new institutions were established. It was at this time that the foundation, frequently incorporated for distributing largesse to various worthy purposes, came into being. Some of the beneficiaries were institutions dealing with medical research and such public health problems as parasitic disease. In 1902 newspapers like the *New York Sun* amused their readers with skeptical accounts of how scientists had finally discovered the "germ" causing the notorious laziness of the Southern poor white. What Charles W. Stiles and Bailey K. Ashford (one in the United States Public Health Service, the other in the Army) had actually discovered was the fact of widespread hookworm infestation in the South and the possibility of treating

[1] This notion, of course, antedates the invention of modern consumer durables and the subsequent development of the economic theory that, in the long run, individual spending creates more capital than mere prudent individual saving.

it by cheap doses of thymol and Epsom salts. Later, in 1909 Virginian Walter Hines Pages persuaded the elder John D. Rockefeller to support an intensive campaign to get the medication distributed and accepted.[2]

When Andrew Carnegie declared that the self-made man should give away his self-made fortune before he died rather than ruin his heirs by leaving them too rich, he was encouraging continued economic activity among the prosperous as well as among the beneficiaries of endowments intended to encourage the less successful in application and industry.

Besides the development of philanthropy, the late nineteenth-century disquiet expressed itself in the anti-monopoly movement as that appeared in books like *Wealth Against Commonwealth* and in political protests which finally produced the first Federal laws regulating economic activity. In the United States, protest against prevailing economic and political patterns has long employed a rhetoric of hostility to privilege and monopoly. The Declaration of Independence does not expressly say that all men should have equal opportunity, but Americans have often interpreted "created equal" to mean just that. In the late 1820's, for example, the Declaration was invoked to support the demand for free public schools; all children had an equal right to an education. In the 1830's similar reasoning brought voters to agree that a national bank with an exclusive Federal charter and sufficient economic power to keep other banks' credit and currency-issuing practices in line with its own constituted an intolerable monopoly. In

[2]Allan Nevins, *John D. Rockefeller: the Heroic Age of American Enterprise*, Vol. II (New York: Charles Scribner's Sons, 1940), pp. 649-51.

the 1840's and 1850's the partisans of free homesteads on the public lands argued that all Americans had an equal right to a share of the public domain and that refusal to implement that right through a homestead law furthered monopoly of land ownership.

The anti-monopoly cry rose again, though somewhat less loudly, perhaps, in connection with the financial policy of the Civil War period and the deflation which followed. The nation returned to hard money, at the expense of debtor-farmers, or so the farmers thought. In the struggle for cheaper money (whether paper or silver) which occurred between the resumption of specie (actually gold) payments in 1876 and the final defeat of the inflationists twenty years later, much of the dispute centered on the contention that hard money, that is, a currency based on a firmly maintained gold reserve, made it so difficult for new entrepreneurs to borrow in order to become competitors that monopoly was encouraged. True, the supply of money did expand through an increase in credit extended to businessmen by the state banks and this facilitated the exchange of goods and services, but it is also true that the farmers could not easily avail themselves of such substitutes for currency since their credit was insufficient.

The anti-monopoly theme continued to be heard during the many years of dispute that finally produced the Interstate Commerce Commission Act of 1887 and the Sherman Anti-Trust Act of 1890. During the decades after the Civil War, concentration of economic power tended to increase. Enterprises grew larger. One enterprise was joined to another. Men added directorship to directorship, share to share, company to company. New kinds of economic organization were devised and older ones were adapted in order to make the concentration of control more effective. Railroads, industrial companies, steamship lines, banks—all tended to pass into the hands of men who did not generally found but were skillful in securing control of companies. The railroads, particularly, since they had been so recklessly financed and often so exploited by their promoters, tended to fall into the hands of financiers who could provide the new money the lines needed to improve their physical plant and who could enforce reorganization of their operations and their corporate structures.

In the 1870's railroads were the inland farmer's only practical means of getting his crops to market and usually there was but one road available. The farmer could ship at the rates charged, or he could let his wheat rot. Farmers turned to politics, trying to get the community to intervene on their side. During the '70's, many Western states did adopt laws which tried to deal with both the level of freight rates and the procedure by which those rates were set. Such legislation aroused great indignation among people like E. L. Godkin of the New York *Nation*, who spoke for the "better element," for those who wanted politicians to keep their hands out of the public till and their laws out of men's private business. The laws which farmers' pressure had secured were invalidated; in a series of decisions, the Supreme Court found that the Federal government had exclusive power to regulate interstate commerce and therefore the laws which the states had adopted to regulate the railroads were unconstitutional. Farmers refused to let that be the last word, however. Shippers, who could not influence railroad management to lower rates for them as the railroads had for some of their larger competitors, joined the opposition to the roads, to their monopoly power and their assistance to the larger entrepreneurs. As a result of years of agitation, the Federal government finally acted: Congress passed the Interstate Commerce Commission Act of 1887. This law forbade a number of abuses, notably, secret rebates lowering published rates for favored shippers, as well as charging the same price for hauling freight a short distance as for hauling it a longer distance along the same route.

Federal action was ineffective. The interstate commerce law proved impossible to enforce in the face of recalcitrant railroad management, shippers too timid to complain of abuses, legal procedures seemingly designed to procure delay, and the Federal courts' willingness to interpret the law in the roads' favor. Nevertheless, this ineffective law opened the way for a new relationship between the government and the economy in the United States. Again, for our purposes, this is of only incidental significance. Our interest is in the anti-monopoly theme and its relation to the secular phase of the multi-faceted paradox of effort. That theme appears strongly in the ideas of Henry George, whose proposal for a single tax won many converts.[3] The anti-monopoly note may be heard in the writings of people like Henry Demarest Lloyd and, later, Ida Tarbell, who described how one group of entrepreneurs contrived to establish control over the oil industry (often, incidentally, by securing rebates which the interstate commerce act had forbidden, and so gaining advantages over its competitors).

Like Henry George himself, few of those who wrote indignant accounts of how competition was being smoth-

[3] George wanted taxation limited to one levy which would take from the individual all increase in the value of land—land only, not the buildings or other improvements made on it—which occurred because of social progress: the growth of towns, the development of transportation, etc.

ered seemed much aware that the free competition they so valued operated to produce the monopoly they deplored. If competition were perfect (the followers of Adam Smith admitted that it never could be) the most effective competitor should be able to eliminate his rivals; by competing, he would secure a monopoly. The ultimate outcome of maintaining a free field for economic effort would be a situation in which concentration of ownership or control would limit the field within which ingenuity and endeavor could be effective.

Few if any Americans realized this; they believed that the organization of the economy was tending toward monopoly because human law was being violated. The anti-monopoly argument finally convinced Congress; three years after it adopted the Interstate Commerce Commission law in 1887, it passed the Sherman Anti-Trust Act. That statute was so loosely phrased that only the courts could give its language concrete meaning, and the Supreme Court tended to decide that Congress had not really meant to reverse the trend toward concentration of economic power.

Nevertheless, like the Interstate Commerce Commission Act, the Sherman Anti-Trust Act marked a major departure in American policy. In however restricted and ineffectual a way, the Federal government was now intervening in the economic process. It was thus acknowledged that the immutable natural laws of economics needed human guidance, for those laws, left to operate without legislative check or supervision, did not perpetuate what was considered to be the most desirable situation. Slowly, after 1890, the Federal government would come to exert a greater influence on the operation of the national economy. Then, instead of functioning merely as keeper of order, enforcer of contracts, and protector of property, the Federal government would, on occasion, use its power in order to weight the scales of social influence on the side of the weaker party. But in 1890 this development—illustrated by the adoption of laws to protect workers in the right to organize—lay far in the future.

It was during the last three decades of the nineteenth century that American trade unionism developed its characteristic social outlook. Between 1870 and the outbreak of the First World War, the labor movement in the United States had three important groups of organizations: the railroad brotherhoods, the Knights of Labor, and the Federation of Trades and Labor Unions, which became the modern American Federation of Labor (AFL). Later, dissident labor groups like the Industrial Workers of the World (I.W.W.) appeared. The dissident groups challenged both the tactics and the basic premises of the larger unions, but the challenge they presented was smothered, largely as the result of prosecution during World War I.

The railroad brotherhoods need not occupy us long. They were set up as much to provide insurance for their members as to act as collective bargaining agents: since early railroading was too dangerous a business to allow profitable commercial insurance of engineers', firemen's, brakemen's, and conductors' lives, their families would be entirely unprotected against hazards unless the men combined to set up insurance funds of their own. In 1877, when the period of economic depression which began in 1873 hit bottom, brotherhood members did walk off their trains in protest against repeated wage cuts. Other workers on the railroads engaged in brief and very violent strikes at the same time.[4] These strikes have been memorialized by the

---

[4] Pittsburgh was in rioters' hands for several days until Federal troops were brought in to restore order.

frowning bastard-medieval armories which still stand in
many of our large cities. Ever more often after 1877, the
Federal government was called in, or moved on its own
initiative, to preserve order in situations where employees
struck, employers refused to deal with their organizations,
and violence grew as union men fought against strike-
breakers, voluntary or employer-procured, in order to save
their jobs.

Often organizations, which expressed the most concili-
atory outlook in their constitutions and other formal statements of purpose, nevertheless showed themselves wholly
willing to fight for their bread and butter. This was true
both of the railroad brotherhoods, as has been shown, and
of the Knights of Labor. After 1877, however, the brotherhoods turned their backs on militancy. They held aloof not
only from the labor movement as a whole, but even from
organizations emerging among other workers on the railroads.

The Knights of Labor, too, contradicted pronouncements
by action—and continued to do so. The Knights was organized as a secret society in 1869 by Uriah S. Stephens,
garment cutter by apprenticeship and friend of Oliver
Hudson Kelley, who founded another, less secret but
longer-lived organization, the Patrons of Husbandry, more
generally known as the Grange. Both societies, as well as
fraternal orders—the Elks, Moose, and Odd Fellows,[5] for

[5] As we discuss the decades after the Civil War, we must remember
that what seems like stability to us in mid-twentieth century was, some
eighty years earlier, a disturbing experience of unremitting change. After
all, one of the best statements of what we consider to be the peculiar
psychological dilemma of our time, the obsolescence of values for which
we have found no adequate replacement, may be seen in the Victorian
poet, Matthew Arnold, who wrote, in his "Grande Chartreuse" that men
were

> "Wandering between two worlds, one dead,
> The other powerless to be born."

example—can be understood as a response to alienation. Kelley, indeed, was impelled to organize the Grange by the isolation, as well as the poverty, which he had witnessed in the post-Civil War South. Such associations bear witness to men's desire for a relatedness to themselves, to each other, and to their work which an increasingly mobile and atomized society no longer provided.[6]

Both the Grange and the Knights of Labor soon began to work for the special economic interests of their members as well as for their psychological comfort. The Noble Order of the Knights of Labor used the rhetoric of fraternalism. It denied that there was any real clash of interest among social classes. It accepted employers as members. Indeed, its local assemblies, whose members might belong to a single craft, to many crafts, or to no craft at all, accepted any man or woman, white or Negro, who worked—provided that he were not a banker, pawnbroker, stock gambler, or liquor dealer. Brewery workers were eligible, however; apparently beer "didn't count." The Order, which had an elaborate ritual and gave its officers grandiloquent titles, was headed by Grand Master Terence V. Powderly,[7] who looked imposing and delivered orations demonstrating how all true Americans were working people and urging the men who worked as employers to arbitrate their differences with the men who worked as their employees.

Although the Knights said it believed in social harmony, it acted on its motto: "An injury to one is an injury to all."

[6] In *The Labor Movement in the United States, 1860-1895* (New York: Appleton, 1929), Norman Ware points out that one important officer in the Knights was also a member of the Order of the Golden Cross, grand senior sagamore of the Improved Order of Red Men, and a Mason of high degree. Powderly was a Mason, too, and honorary member of G.A.R. posts in seventeen different states.

[7] Stephens had resigned in 1879. Two years later, he quarreled with Powderly and disappeared from the annals of the Order. *See* Ware, *op. cit.*, pp. 23-26.

Its locals went out on strike. It used the withdrawal of purchasing power as an economic weapon, and Knights of Labor boycotts were particularly successful where cigars, beer, and other commodities bought by men were concerned. Knights of Labor strikes were effective too, especially on the railroads where the organization attracted non-operating employees.

By the middle 1880's, the Knights seemed to be a real power, able to elect political officers (Powderly was Mayor of Scranton from 1878 to 1882) and to push legislation on even the Federal level (the Knights took credit for the establishment of a Federal Bureau of Labor Statistics in 1884 and for the adoption of a law forbidding the importation of laborers who were under contract to work out the cost of their passage). In 1886, however, the lower-level leadership of the Knights was drawn into violence, particularly in the strikes of mechanics and maintenance men on the Western railroads [8] which followed the economic downturn of 1883. Writs of injunction forbidding the strikes on penalty of summary punishment for contempt of court, as well as the importation of strike-breakers and the use of armed force, finally defeated the strikers.

Defeat on the railroads meant the collapse of the Knights' campaign to organize unskilled and semiskilled workers. The organization also suffered because, quite contrary to the facts, it was charged with being involved in the Haymarket riots in Chicago, where several people—policemen and bystanders—were killed when dynamite bombs were thrown at a meeting called to protest the arrest of strikers at the McCormick Reaper plant. That strike was linked to a planned demonstration and a concerted drive for the

[8] Ibid., pp. 303-11.

eight-hour standard working day. Widespread anger roused
by the Haymarket incident deprived the eight-hour movement of what support it had outside the unions, and its
failure further damaged the Knights although, ironically,
Powderly did not approve of the project and had prevented
the Knights from giving effective support to the May Day
demonstration.

About this time, more and more of the skilled craftsmen
who accounted for a large segment of the Knights' membership came to believe that they were being asked to take
an unreasonable number of risks, to participate in too many
boycotts and even strikes, for the benefit of the less skilled.
In 1881 the Federation of Trades and Labor Unions was set
up as a separate organization of national unions of skilled
workers (stone cutters, household stove molders, printers,
and some building craftsmen), combining unions which
had existed before and alongside of the Knights. After 1886
increasing numbers of the skilled workers in the Knights
of Labor moved over into the rival camp. Without the
stability and the funds they had contributed, the Knights'
unskilled and semiskilled membership dwindled as rapidly
as it had swelled.

By 1892 the Knights had all but disappeared as a significant labor organization. In a rueful post-mortem, Powderly
wrote: "Advising against strikes, we have been in the midst
of them. . . . Urging important reforms, we have concentrated on petty disputes. Unpolitical, we have been forced
into political action." [9] Preaching class harmony, to carry
on in his rhythm, the Knights were involved in violence (as
in the strike against the Missouri-Pacific in 1886) [10] and

[9] Ibid., p. 375.
[10] Ruth Allen, *The Great Southwest Strike* (Austin, Texas: University
of Texas, 1942).

won at least temporary economic success by using a class-oriented technique, the boycott of consumer goods. For in the 1880's, certain commodities were manufactured for a specifically working-class market and union men's refusal to buy such goods could bankrupt a retailer or severely injure a manufacturer.

The Knights' successor, the American Federation of Labor, did not attempt to conduct any consistent long-term campaign to draw large numbers of semiskilled and unskilled workers into the labor movement. (It is interesting to note how the United Mine Workers, which did try to organize all workers in its industry rather than any single craft, wavered between the Knights and the Federation until it finally chose the AFL.) Since the Federation was founded in 1886, no disinterested observer has charged the main sector of the American labor movement with any coherent long-range social viewpoint. Like other Americans, most union leaders have thought they lived in the best of all possible worlds. They wanted more of what the world had to offer; they were generally quite innocent of desire to change it.

One can, of course, cite leaders and organizations that did not hold this view, most notable perhaps being Eugene V. Debs and the I.W.W. Debs was a dissenter from the philosophy of the railroad brotherhoods when he attempted to organize the unorganized. He tried to bring all railroad workers into one union and had made considerable progress toward that end when the American Railway Union, as the new organization was called, struck in sympathy with the workers who made Pullman cars.[11] Debs was jailed for

[11] Debs, a brakeman by occupation, had helped found the Brotherhood of Railway Trainmen. *See also* Almont Lindsey, *Pullman Strike* (Chicago: University of Chicago Press, 1942).

violating an injunction forbidding the sympathy strike, and the American Railway Union, like the men and women at Pullman, was defeated. In jail, meanwhile, Debs read the books which converted him to socialism.

The I.W.W., with its syndicalist orientation,[12] was thoroughly contemptuous of the "coffin societies" of the AFL. (Many Federation unions paid death benefits, a practice which had a stabilizing effect on membership but which may also have tended to discourage militancy.) It is not really farfetched to label the I.W.W. the most alienated wing of the American labor movement, for it scorned accepted institutions, such as voting at elections, since it considered elections a sham, and looked down on respected persons: sheriffs, millionaires, parsons, and labor leaders like Sam Gompers. Like the Knights of Labor, the I.W.W. tried to organize the unskilled and semiskilled laborers in lumbering, mining, and agriculture, occupations where the field of operations was remote, the work hard, and the work force tough and untrammeled (migratory farm workers were roving men, in those days, not moving families). Many I.W.W. members were literal aliens in every community where they worked. The One Big Union [13] was their only home.

It has been said that the typical hero of the great American novelists is the alienated man, the man without a community. If this is so, it may help explain the most legendary aura which still surrounds the I.W.W. The prevalence of

12 Unlike the socialists, the syndicalists desired to establish a loosely organized society in which local workers' organizations would operate an extremely decentralized economy and there would be no need for coercive political government or, indeed, for any government at all.

13 This slogan was revived and used by the CIO in the 1930's. Wherever there is any vigor in the American labor movement, I.W.W. catchwords and songs are heard.

rootless men among its membership accounts for both its long-run ineffectiveness and for its paradoxically spectacular successes. Before Gandhi, and with less formal philosophic argument, the I.W.W. used the technique of civil disobedience to secure such civil rights as freedom of speech: in labor struggles in small Far Western towns particularly, its members flocked in to help their fellows, courted arrest, and so crowded the jails that the taxpayers found keeping them locked up too expensive. The organization was thoroughly hated, accordingly, both by the employers it attacked and by the "official" trade union movement that it jeered at and showed to be inadequate. One does not wonder that the I.W.W. should have been one of the first dissident groups to be assailed when the United States entered the First World War and that the measures taken against its members were particularly brutal.

The I.W.W. and the AFL did have one point in common, however: both were deeply distrustful of government intervention to protect workingmen for both believed that government belonged to labor's enemies.[14] (So much apparently of the Marxist socialism that Gompers said he had once embraced and then abandoned, he continued to accept.)

Although the Federation proclaimed its respectability by disclaiming any socialist purpose or ideas and particularly by disclaiming any intention to play a role in party politics, and although it wanted wages and working conditions determined solely by workers' organizations bargaining with

[14] Gompers and Vincent St. John of the I.W.W. made strikingly similar statements on this point at a hearing before the Industrial Commission which Congress set up to inquire into the causes of the labor unrest which was so prevalent in the decade before 1914. *See* Senate Document No. 415, 64th Congress, 1st Session, 1916.

their employers, the Federation and its constituent unions were pushed into concern with legislation. The AFL agreed with spokesmen for social welfare agencies and sociologist Robert Hunter, who in 1904 made one of the the first relatively objective inquiries into poverty in the United States. Like Mathew Carey, the Philadelphia publisher and economist who made a far more informal study early in the 1830's, Hunter pointed out that the income of the unskilled worker, and therefore his ability to keep above the poverty line, depended more on the movement of the business cycle than on his own industriousness.[15] Unskilled laborers, and especially the increasing number of women workers, could not protect themselves against unemployment or the pressure of excess labor supplies on wage rates. They were helpless individually and usually unable to band into effective unions; hence such workers needed protection by the community.

The Federation, therefore, supported laws to limit working hours, to fix minimum wages for women, to bar them from work in dangerous trades or under dangerous conditions, and to raise the age at which children could be hired (one should remember that until 1930 the Bureau of the Census counted everyone over ten years old as a member of the labor force.)

Furthermore, as a result of court action, particularly the

[15] In his *Appeal to the Wealthy of the Land* (Philadelphia, 1833), Carey pointed out that the most industrious laborer could earn no more than $198.00 a year and that it cost $194.50 to feed, clothe, and shelter a family of four. Robert Hunter reported that it took a minimum of $460 a year to keep a family of four and that the average laborer earned between $375 and $450. *See* Hunter, *Poverty* (New York: The Macmillan Co., 1904). Both writers note the difficulty of securing accurate information on earnings. The resemblance between the situations they observed is striking, despite the great changes which had occurred between 1833 and the early 1900's.

issuing of writs of injunction to forbid strikes and to make picketing ineffective, the Federation was also obliged to recognize that unless government did intervene, did at least admit that freedom to bargain through labor unions was a right deserving legal protection, workers' organizations would exist only on sufferance. For employer groups had more than an economic advantage; the community, insofar as the law expresses the community, was on their side. Union men frequently were held to have broken the law when they struck: picketing could easily be called trespass, or intimidation of people who wanted to work on the terms the strikers had rejected. Unions and their members were found to be breaking the law when they refused to buy or to work on goods made by an anti-union employer (the courts declared boycotts to constitute conspiracy in restraint of trade often enough to make unions drop general use of what had been a useful weapon).

Particularly important to workers was legal acceptance of the strike to compel an employer to bargain. Refusal to deal with unions is still rather common, but it was all but the rule in large-scale industry until the 1930's. Without legislative recognition of collective bargaining as a legal right (and court approval of that legislation as constitutional), American unions continued to function in a shadowy area where legal tolerance might shrink to the measure of the Supreme Court's decision in the Coronado case.[16] Though the court decided here that the mere existence of a union did not violate the Sherman Anti-Trust Act, other decisions made it appear that most union actions did constitute such a violation.

[16] *United Mine Workers* vs. *Coronado Coal Co.*, 259 U.S. 344 (1922); *Coronado Coal Co.* vs. *United Mine Workers*, 268 U.S. 295 (1925).

Consequently, in order to secure freedom to act, the AFL was pushed toward the very participation in campaigns which its leaders disapproved. The Federation avoided commitment and urged its members to vote for labor's friends, whatever their party, and so to punish labor's enemies. Its success was small, but that is not our concern; here we are dealing with the somewhat paradoxical situation of a trade union movement conscientiously non-political and unconcerned with social ideas being driven to use a political tactic though it did not organize a party with a program offering a genuine alternative to the consensus which contemporary scholars in political science understand to have governed America's development.

Neither in the early years of the twentieth century nor afterward did the American labor movement offer an explicit alternative to the prevailing political faith. American unions have often behaved violently, but rarely have they been consistently militant. Nevertheless, even while the labor movement was proclaiming its acceptance of the world as it was, its behavior indicated significant departures from that allegiance. Hidden behind the façade of concentration on Gompers' slogan, "More Now," was the notion that most workmen could not become wealthy or even small employers by thrift and individual industry. Individual diligence could not achieve rising wages and shorter workdays. Only by joining with others could workers set standards of performance at reasonable levels—levels which would make certain that they were not beguiled by manipulation of piecework rates into laboring at a depleting pace, in order to earn a wage that would provide at least the customary standard of living. Studies made in non-union plants have shown how social pressure within the working force operates even there to keep individual output at what the group considers a livable rate; nevertheless, only organization can make that sort of pressure effective in situations where employees are easy to replace and employers can hire industrial engineers to manipulate the speed of assembly lines. Insofar as unions are successful, they do tend to limit output and to put brakes on individual achievement. Those brakes work, so union theorists argue, to restrict output in order to make sure labor gets a just reward.

We have discussed two aspects of the uneasiness that some Americans felt as they confronted their world. We have at least implied that their active expression of uneasiness had some impact. Changes in opinion slowly became evident and those changes were reflected in legislative gestures toward the regulation of business practices and toward the protection of the economically disadvantaged. Between 1894 and 1914, lagging behind most industrialized European countries, some industrial states acted to adopt workmen's compensation laws, and so make it profitable for employers to install safety devices in order to lower the incidence and the cost of accidental injury. They introduced minimum wage laws for women, limited the working day, gave widows pensions so that they could maintain homes for their children, and even raised the school-leaving age.

Measures of this sort were among the objectives of what is known as the Progressive movement, which may in one sense be taken as the political expression of a growing public dissatisfaction with the world which unrestrictedly money-oriented men had made. Within both the Democratic and the Republican parties, the entrenched leaders were dedicated to rocking no boats and resolving no problems. In both parties, factions emerged which opposed the leadership. These insurgents gradually increased in influence until they were able, at least briefly in 1912, to disrupt the Republican party and to exert sufficient pressure upon the Democratic party to persuade both its urban bosses and its old-line Southern supporters that a progressive candidate would have a good chance of winning the presidency.

Meanwhile, however, a considerable number of Americans had grown dissatisfied with the rather foggy aspirations of the Progressives. For progressivism was a cast of mind or, at best, a series of separate programs—reorganization of municipal government, for instance, or the introduction of the direct primary; progressivism had neither a consistent economic theory nor an effective separate party organization. By the early 1900's a number of these dissatisfied Americans—some in the trade union movement, where they were an appreciable minority and many intellectuals outside—were finding socialism less frightening than it had seemed in the 1880's (or does today). With Debs as its leader, the Socialist party began to record an increasing number of votes in national elections, to elect a couple of members to Congress, to send a few representatives to state legislatures, and to install a fair number of municipal officers. This very small success roused a wholly disproportionate concern among conservatives. By 1912 Henry Adams and his brother Brooks [17] were certain that the success of even progressivism portended disaster—and this fear may help to explain the peculiarly unbridled character of the attack on civil liberty during the First World War, an attack we shall discuss in the next chapter.

The character of the new laws adopted, particularly be-

[17] John A. Garraty, *Henry Cabot Lodge* (New York: Alfred A. Knopf, 1953), p. 293.

tween 1904 and 1914, indicates that organized workers were being heard by legislators and also that the neglect of politics by the "better element" was tending to diminish. As prosperous, efficient, and earnest citizens began to realize that slipshod government was expensive and that government for the provision of patronage to support political machines did not produce even the few services which were considered necessary, they began to demand reforms which would make government honest and representative. The beginnings of the substitution of merit, measured by competitive examination, for party regularity as a qualification for public office had been made in 1883, when Congress passed a law applying the merit system to the Federal civil service. But the advocates of political decency found themselves involved in contradiction, as Lincoln Steffens pointed out as early as 1903. Honest, efficient government was indeed desirable, particularly in cities where ineffective policing, dirty streets, and inadequate schools were all too common. Yet impartial enforcement of existing laws might well lower profits, as in the instance of sanitary regulations and the return on tenement property. Awarding public utility franchises on terms best for a city might deprive persons of opportunity to make considerable fortunes. The desire, sometimes the need, for special favors tended, therefore, to weaken enthusiasm for consistently honest municipal government. This fact, and the better element's inevitable loss of interest in the humdrum tasks whose performance is actually the price of political effectiveness, help account for the ever-repeated ousting of reform adminstrations by political machines, a phenomenon which has continued into mid-twentieth century.

Between the end of the Civil War and the 1880's, the

United States saw the apotheosis of individual striving. The artist looked at the world which such individualism was making and he asserted that it was not good. Though less prescient than the artist, philanthropists, political reformers, trade unionists, even certain sociologists who did not agree with William Graham Sumner, looked at this world and grew increasingly aware of its deficiencies. But even people who conceded the need for laws and legal machinery to deal with child labor, for example, did not often relate the problems of which they were aware to the single-minded concentration on money-making which continued to be regarded as the most proper occupation of the American man.

Saving Democracy 8

IN THE FOREGOING chapters, we have seen how alienation and loneliness continued to develop along with industrialization. Alienation was not a term much used in the last decades of the nineteenth century, but what it represented existed and was considered good, as we have seen, proof of independence. Those who found small merit in what was considered a social advance were a minority, but one slowly growing more influential.

Standing alone might be thought to be a barrier to the development of conformity, but this did not prove to be true. The roots of the trend toward conforming are to be found in another aspect of the American past. Small settlements during succeeding stages of the development of this country contributed to conformity, and if conformity has been more oppressive in the American small town than in England, say, it may be because the enormous size of our country tended to dwarf people and town, making the town's inhabitants more dependent on each other for psychological security when faced with the vastness of their world. In such a community, mores and morality, being the cake of custom which holds the community together in comfort, must necessarily be uniform, and the individual conforms not only in order to be part of the community but in order to have the approval of the community which contributes to shape his own super-ego. He conforms to prove to himself that he is good—and sometimes that he is as good as the next man.

As we leave the nineteenth century and turn to World War I, we begin our sketch of the development of what may be termed the *new* conformity. The entire story of America's participation in the Great War points up paradoxes both of our foreign policy and of our leadership. After 1898 and our triumph over Spain, successive administrations, as we shall see, tried to make the United States a power in the world without committing their country to bearing the cost and consequences of assuming such status. And this attempt to have power without paying power's price was to continue after the war and down to the 1940's.

Since 1789, the United States had consistently sought to avoid being drawn into European quarrels. It failed during the great struggle between France and England at the opening of the century, but its experience in the War of 1812 only increased the desire for isolation. It is interesting to note at this point that before James Monroe, in 1823, enunciated the doctrine that bears his name, Jefferson influenced him toward emphasizing our aloofness, pointing out that the world was divided into two spheres and that it was impossible for the United States to take any responsibility for the fate of liberty in the European sphere, dominated as that was after the Napoleonic Wars by restored reactionary monarchies.

The principal maritime powers kept their wars local after 1815, and the United States was thus able to maintain its isolation; it was free to pursue its own development without becoming enmeshed in world struggles for power. When it

fell into civil conflict, the chief European powers, after a
gesture or so toward mediation, remained on their own side
of the Atlantic.[1]

During the last quarter of the nineteenth century, the
principal European nations extended their struggle for
power throughout the world. The United States took no
significant part in that struggle. It dabbled. Its stance may
well parallel the paradox in the nursery rhyme:

> Mother may I go out to swim?
> Yes, my darling daughter,
> Hang your clothes on a hickory limb,
> But don't go near the water.

The United States wrangled with the Germans over control of the Samoan islands, for example, and settled the dispute by dividing the territory in 1899. (Since Hawaii had
long been an American sphere of influence, occasionally
encroached upon by Britain, to be sure, Hawaii's annexation
in 1898 was no departure from the traditional policy which
renounced European involvement, not territorial aggran-
dizement.) Even after victory in the War with Spain made

---

[1] To be sure, many interests in Britain did not delight in the existence
of the United States, but when the opportunity arose to harm the
country while the United States was engaged in the Civil War, other
British interests made it impossible for hostile groups to take advantage
of that opportunity; aristocratic sympathies and the need for cotton were
defeated by superior Northern propaganda, the opportunities for profit
in selling arms to the North, and the accumulated supply of cotton
which prevented real shortage until fairly late in the war when Northern
victory seemed probable. The subsequent dispute between the United
States and Britain over British responsibility for the damage done by
Confederate raiders built in British shipyards was acrimonious enough,
but it was successfully referred to arbitration in 1871. Some British statesmen continued to speak superciliously of the United States, and numbers
of American politicians strove for Irish votes by twisting the lion's tail
in their speeches, but relations between the two countries were tolerably
amicable.

it reasonable for the United States to assume the role of a great power, American administrations were readier to move on the Asian than on the European stage.

In dealing with Pacific affairs and the rising power of Japan, Theodore Roosevelt allowed himself to be persuaded to act in the Russo-Japanese War as peacemaker when Britain and France each decided that its particular ally needed protection—Japan against an impending exhaustion of its resources, Russia against the threat of revolution.

After the Peace of Portsmouth was concluded in 1905, Roosevelt and his sucessor, William Howard Taft, contrived to guide American policy toward Japan along a path twisting between wordy assertion of American rights and cautious refusal to back that assertion by display of force. Thus, in spite of repeated declarations concerning the right of all nations to trade freely and on equal terms in China, the United States made no attempt to secure its asserted right by the use of ships and troops, as European nations had, and in the secret Root-Takahira agreements of 1908 went so far as pledging maintenance of the *status quo* in the Pacific and hence, implicitly, recognizing Japan's special position in China.

Meanwhile, the United States raised a small voice in the European concert. In response to a request from the Kaiser, Theodore Roosevelt persuaded Britain and France to call a conference at Algeciras in 1906 to settle the affairs of Morocco and the dispute between France and Germany which had arisen about those affairs. (The American delegate, incidentally, consistently voted against the Germans at the conference.) The United States did sign the agreement reached at Algeciras, an agreement which some his-

torians think postponed World War I,[2] but the Senate
ratified that treaty only after it had specifically declared
that its action did not oblige the United States to enforce
the treaty's provisions nor did ratification constitute a prece-
dent for future American participation in European affairs.

When World War I did break out in 1914, and particularly when German use of the submarine gave maritime
warfare a new dimension, the Wilson administration found
itself faced with dilemmas implicit in the nation's isolationist
bias. It insisted on its rights of trade as a neutral. And since
neither belligerent respected those rights, it could maintain isolationism only by renouncing them. This, economically, it could not afford to do. It opted against Germany
although the British violation of neutral rights was almost
as great as her opponent's. In April, 1917, the United States
entered the war and the era of actual isolation was over.

The United States went into the war with the slogan
"Make the World Safe for Democracy." But as the world's
greatest democracy fought in democracy's defense, it depleted the liberties of its own citizens both by directly
repressive action and by a thoroughgoing propaganda campaign.

The United States has a kind of equality unknown in
European countries: there is great flexibility between classes
both in mobility and in attitude; for example, a lack of for-
mality has long been characteristic of Americans in their
dealings with each other. This acceptance of equality makes
for a lack of those picturesque traditional differentiations
which Henry James sought and found in the European
scene. Where there is little differentiation, non-conformity

[2] George E. Mowry, *Era of Theodore Roosevelt* (New York: Harper
& Brothers, 1958), p. 196.

may be considered a threat ("Who does he think he is?" "He's no better than me!") and provokes a repression which is a denial of liberty.

Almost a hundred years earlier, Alexis de Tocqueville had declared, in some degree as a result of what he saw in the United States, that liberty and equality were at least partially incompatible. Liberty, he thought, was in especial danger in a warlike democracy.[3]

The United States did not regard itself as a warlike country although as a nation it was born in war, grew to strength amidst the wars of others, gained territory by war, and preserved its national existence by war. In the years between 1916 and 1923, the behavior of many Americans and of their government supported De Tocqueville's contention. The actions of administrative officials and the conduct of private individuals all assaulted the right to think as one chose and to speak one's thought without penalty, legal or social.

The threat to civil liberty was not ignored by the President. Wilson is reported to have said to Frank Cobb of the *New York World:* "Once lead this people into war . . . and the spirit of ruthless brutality will enter into the very fibre of our national life, infecting Congress, the courts, the policeman, the man in the street." [4]

Yet Wilson signed the Sedition and Espionage Acts of 1917 and 1918 with no protest and, so far as is known, did not disagree with the manner in which they were enforced.

---

[3] "Equality," he wrote, "awakens in men several propensities dangerous to freedom . . . neglect of forms, undervaluing of private rights." *Democracy in America,* trans. by Henry Reeve, Vol. IV (London, 1840), p. 336.
[4] Mark Sullivan, *Our Times,* Vol. V. (New York: Charles Scribner's Sons, 1933), p. 474.

His awareness of the probable effect of the war upon civil liberty makes his acquiescence, particularly in the post-Armistice phase of suppression, appear all the more surprising. Wilson was the professional scholar in politics, the only academic political scientist ever to become President. Yet not only did he do little if anything to check excessive zeal in furthering national unity during the war; he showed no humane concern after the fact: several of the people imprisoned for violation of wartime sedition laws, including Eugene V. Debs, were not released until after Warren G. Harding had taken office. The case of Debs is particularly interesting. Wilson's second Attorney General, A. Mitchell Palmer, was at first opposed to releasing Debs after the Armistice. Freeing the Socialist leader, Palmer thought, would help those who were opposed to ratifying the Versailles Treaty. Palmer changed his mind, however, but Wilson then overruled him.[5]

Wilson appears to have been directed by conviction not only of his own rectitude (so that differing with his policy became an offense against morality) but of the special character of the war in which the United States was engaged. To him, American participation in World War I was no mere matter of national interest, of fighting because Americans' right to trade freely had been infringed and because German victory would erect obstacles to American political and economic advancement. To Wilson, America's role in the war meant the opportunity for a just peace which would, once and forever, break the cycle of wars being ended by settlements which contained the germs of future wars. For this end and for creating the machinery for keep-

[5] Stanley Coben, *A. Mitchell Palmer: Politician* (New York: Columbia University Press, 1963), pp. 199-202.

ing that peace, Wilson was willing to have civil liberities treated as matters of secondary importance.

The push toward conformity which the war gave the United States appears in two phases: manipulative and coercive—molding opinion and punishing the expression of dissent. Manipulation was more novel than coercion. For the first time, an American government created a large-scale propaganda agency in order to direct public opinion at home as well as to try to influence opinion abroad. The new agency was called the Committee on Public Information; its director was George Creel, who had been a rather well-known Western Progressive, and the committee was able to employ many techniques of contemporary advertising.[6] Belief that a domestic propaganda campaign was necessary rested, among other facts, on the large number of people of German origin in the United States, many of whom expressed affection for the Fatherland in musical and athletic organizations, and on the considerable strength which political dissidence had achieved by 1912. Wilson, as we have observed, owed his very election to this dissent: the division within the Republican party had led to the secession of Theodore Roosevelt's Progressives and made Wilson's plurality possible.

Debs had polled 987,000 votes for the Socialists, mean-

[6] By 1914, relatively modern techniques were being used for marketing soap, cigarettes, etc.; the first professional public relations specialists were being employed by industrial concerns to create suitable "images." For discussion of the Creel Committee, see James R. Mock and Cedric Larson, *Words That Won the War* (Princeton, N. J.: Princeton University Press, 1939). In Creel's autobiography, *Rebel at Large* (New York: Putnam, 1947), he takes particular pride in how cheaply he carried on his campaign, as compared to the operation of the Office of War Information during World War II, and how little "nonsense" he tolerated from foreigners in the name of "cultural relations": European film exhibitors, he says, showed American propaganda or could rent no popular Mary Pickford films (see p. 169).

while. Some of the dissent was pacifist in orientation. When war came the Socialist party continued faithful to its internationalist tradition although some of the intellectuals in its ranks did leave the party in order to support the war. Pacifist sentiment continued to exist outside the Socialist party, and many people believed that sentiment to be much stronger than it actually was. Therefore the Sedition and Espionage Acts were adopted. So far as law could prevent men from speaking their minds about war, these laws did so. The Espionage Act of 1917 forbade false reports or statements made with intent to interfere with the operation of the armed forces, or to obstruct recruiting or the draft. Apparently this measure did not go far enough. As Attorney General Gregory reported to Congress, people making disloyal statements were provoking patriotic citizens to violence. To prevent disorder, he urged that Congress modify the law. His request was complied with: in May, 1918, Congress added a number of new offenses to the Espionage Act. These included hindering bond sales; using language derogatory to the Constitution, the flag, the uniform of the armed services, the form of government of the United States; favoring the enemy in words; curtailing war production; or advocating any such acts.

As a result, men were prosecuted and punished for words rather than actions, and for the presumed intent of their words rather than for any demonstrated consequences of them. It became criminal to criticize the Red Cross, to say that the sinking of merchant vessels was legal under international law (as indeed it had been), to advocate financing the war by taxation rather than bond issues, even to discourage women from knitting socks by saying that those socks did not reach the soldiers for whom they were intended.

The temper in which prosecutions were carried on under these laws—2,000 cases were brought—is illustrated by a statement of Judge Wade in charging an Iowa jury: the law, he said, was needed to deal with "the few who will not heed the judgment of the 95 per cent, [the few] who assume to know more than all the others put together." [7]

Private citizens were encouraged to organize for the purpose of keeping watch on, and informing the authorities about, suspicious activities by their neighbors.

In addition to judicial law enforcement, administrative fiat, in effect, came into play. The office of Postmaster General had gone to Albert Burleson of Texas, a skillful dispenser of political patronage and no man to value the expression of dissent as essential to democratic government. The Postmaster General has authority to determine a periodical's eligibility for second-class mailing privileges: without that subsidy, few nationally circulated journals could exist. Suspension of that privilege for even a few weeks could deplete a weekly paper's treasury; denial was lethal. Suspension and denial both were used against foreign-language newspapers whose content did not meet with government approval and against journals of radical opinion. The old *Masses*, for example, had its second-class privileges suspended.[8] The *Seattle Times-Record* encountered similar treatment, and after the Armistice.

The Espionage Acts made certain matter non-mailable because of its possible effect on the morale of the troops.

[7] Zachariah Chafee, *Free Speech in the United States* (Cambridge, Mass.: Harvard University Press, 1941), p. 56.
[8] James Mock, *Censorship: 1917* (Princeton, N. J.: Princeton University Press, 1941); Chafee, *op. cit.,* pp. 99-104.

The Postmaster General became a kind of political censor as a result, usually acting on the advice of the War Department or the Committee on Public Information. Most of the banned books presented the German side of the war, but some, like Ambrose Bierce's Civil War stories, had been written many years before World War I, and others, like Thorstein Veblen's *Imperial Germany and the Industrial Revolution*, in effect supported the Allied cause.[9]

Manipulation of opinion and legal restrictions on its expression were reinforced (or perhaps made possible) by propagandistic stupidity ranging from rechristening sauerkraut "liberty cabbage" to stopping performances of Wagner's operas and halting secondary-school instruction in the German language. Windows of shops owned by people with German names were broken. Strikers were labeled pro-German and strikes were attacked as unpatriotic.

The I.W.W. particularly was assailed both by legal prosecution and mob violence. Between 1917 and 1920, twenty states and what were then the territories of Alaska and Hawaii adopted "criminal syndicalism" laws, many of which are still in force although their application has been moderated by subsequent Supreme Court decisions. These statutes were generally promoted by organized employers —or large-scale farm operators—approved by a press hostile to the I.W.W., and enthusiastically accepted by legislators affected by hysterical opposition to "radicalism." [10] The criminal syndicalism laws are so phrased as to make the advocacy of opinions or policies a felony; no proof of action

[9] Freud's *Reflections on War and Death* was cited to the Creel Committee by a volunteer informer and Creel promised to call the book to the attention of the authorities (Mock, *op. cit.*, p. 154).

[10] E. F. Dowell, *History of Criminal Syndicalism Legislation in the United States* (Baltimore, Md.: Johns Hopkins University Press, 1939), pp. 18, 24, 45.

is required. Along with the Federal Sedition and Espionage Acts of 1917-18, these state laws can be taken as indicating a rather widespread willingness to make "freedom of speech" mean "freedom to say what is generally acceptable."

A number of prosecutions were brought under state laws, but Federal action was more important. Forty-nine I.W.W. leaders were tried, convicted, and sentenced to terms of ten to twenty years for violating the Espionage Acts.[11]

I.W.W. members in the lumbering and copper-mining industries particularly met not only the customary tactics of refusal to bargain and the procuring of strike-breakers, but also the kind of mob violence represented by the Bisbee deportations (when several hundred copper miners were carted off into the Arizona desert), and by the episode at Centralia, Washington, where an Armistice Day parade ended in a riot around I.W.W. headquarters; a parader was killed and an I.W.W. lumber worker was sadistically lynched.[12]

It was after the Armistice, however, that the new conformity blossomed. By 1919 the Russian Revolution—welcomed with enthusiasm and relief in the United States when it seemed merely a replacement of an ineffectual Tsarist regime by a parliamentary government which would fight more effectively than its embarrassingly absolutist predecessor—had passed into its communist phase. In the United States, fear seemed to rise in inverse proportion to

11 Chafee, *op. cit.*, p. 79.
12 A number of the I.W.W. men who fought to defend their headquarters were tried and sentenced to long prison terms; no one was ever found responsible for the lynching. The facts concerning what actually occurred are obscure, but it is certain that violence was met with violence.

physical remoteness from the source of danger and to the
real weakness of social dissent in America. The fear which
did exist was rationalized largely in terms of the wave of
strikes which affected the economy in 1919 [13] and 1920
when, war demand ending, wages ceased to rise, and the
Federal government had dismantled the boards and com-
missions which had given organized labor some recognition
during the period of wartime industrial mobilization.

It will be remembered that it was found necessary for the
government to take over the railroads in 1917 and operate
them as a single system. It will be remembered, too, that
the Overman Act of 1918 had given the Federal government a wide range of power to keep industry producing.
To Gompers and the American Federation of Labor, the
war situation seemed both a danger and an opportunity.
Anti-labor sentiment in government might deprive unions
of even the limited gains they had made since 1900. But
cooperation with the government might gain for organized
labor a favorable position in respect to the regulatory bodies
which, it was expected, would be set up and, further, might
give the labor movement and its leaders the respectability
which they so desperately craved.

In return for an informal AFL pledge to restrain strikes
during the war, the government established boards, on
which unions were represented, to settle labor disputes and
to establish standards of wages and working conditions, including the eight-hour working day. In this arrangement,
the steel industry did not participate; it successfully refused
to accept the principle of collective bargaining with its
employees and it maintained the basic 72-hour work week,

[13] Between February and November, 1919, some four million workers
were involved in 3,600 strikes. *See* Florence Peterson, *Strikes in the
United States 1880-1936* (U.S. Department of Labor Bulletin No. 651,
Washington, D.C., 1938).

with a 24-hour "turn," that is, a 24-hour working day, when shifts changed, in order to assure continuous operation.

In the 1880's the Amalgamated Iron and Steel Workers had brought highly skilled workers into a craft union so exclusive that it had small place for even the helpers who worked alongside its members; it certainly made no effective effort to bring the unskilled into its organization. Because of this policy, but more importantly because the steel magnates were totally determined to be rid of even the slight counterweight that the Amalgamated represented, the organization failed disastrously when it went out on strike in 1892 at the Homestead plant of the Carnegie Steel Company. Thereafter management governed as it chose. The works councils which were set up during the war, and in which the AFL unions just mentioned did acquire some influence, had little effect on the situation. But after the armistice, a number of AFL unions joined together in a major effort to break into the anti-union fortress of steelmaking.

The steel strike of 1919 failed: the joint organization set up by the unions was unwieldy; the resources the unions could summon were insufficient to fight steel management's money, command of private police forces in company towns, influence on the press and in local politics, and the climate being generated in the United States. All protest was labeled Bolshevism, now, and strikes were the most evident kind of protest, however little the strikers might know or care about social theories.

Private enterprise disposed of the steel strike: the new organization broke up; the men went back to work on the companies' terms;[14] steel management ruled unchecked until

[14] In 1923, after prodding from a generally inert administration, the steel industry finally did shorten the working week.

the 1930's, when depression and a changed political climate gave the CIO its opportunity. The two other important strikes of the period, the bituminous coal miners' walkout in 1919 and the threatened strike of railway men, were dealt with by the government. Wartime legislation continued in force because the United States did not conclude a formal peace with Germany until 1922. Hence the Federal government retained its authority to make certain that there was no interference with the production of necessities. The miners were ordered back to work on penalty of being punished for hampering the war effort. After some resistance, the miners obeyed. Thereafter, the United Mine Workers experienced a long period of defeat and decline, foreshadowing what was to happen to organized labor in general during the 1920's.

The situation of the railway workers was somewhat different. The railroads were returned to exclusive management control in 1919 (to take effect in March, 1920). Workers threatened to strike because their wages had not kept pace with wartime price rises. Fear of governmental action like that taken against the miners, who were enjoined from striking or using their funds to support strikers, kept the railway men on the job. After 1920, management cut wages and attacked the structure of working rules and grievance machinery set up during the period of governmental operation. The men who maintained rolling stock walked out in 1923. Railroad management procured injunctions,[15] unusually sweeping in their terms, which forbade

[15] Injunctions, being writs in equity, can be issued without even hearing both parties in instances where irremediable damage may occur; violation is punishable as contempt of court without jury trial. In labor disputes, this is no longer true; the Norris-LaGuardia Act requires that both sides shall be heard before the writ is issued, that the behavior forbidden be spelled out, and that violators of an injunction be allowed to have a trial by jury.

not only picketing and other action in support of the strike but even discussion of the injunction itself by third parties.

The defeat of these great strikes had political repercussions: Senator Robert M. La Follette ran for President with labor support in 1924. His defeat marked the triumph of conservatism in the 1920's, or perhaps it would be more accurate to say that the failure of La Follette and his supporters marked the collapse of political interest among the people who, during the prewar period, had been concerned with the attempt to establish responsible and representative government and with the effort to secure what we generally call social legislation.

As mentioned earlier, much of the government's action against labor, with the denial of free speech that it entailed, was based upon the fact that the nation was still legally at war. President Wilson had gone abroad as chief negotiator for the United States with the confidence of a leader whose country had no mean ambition for territory. The United States, with its resources intact and its economy vigorous, held the material and moral keys to a just and lasting peace, and Woodrow Wilson was the man who knew how to use those keys. Once again, the eloquent spokesman for democracy behaved rather undemocratically: while peace was being negotiated, Wilson took few party or congressional leaders into his confidence and made little attempt to secure support among newspaper men. Rather, he presented the nation with the *fait accompli*, the Treaty of Versailles as that had been drafted in haste by political leaders soured by vindictiveness, concerned for their positions, and fearful of what storms the Russian Revolution might evoke in their own countries, exhausted as those were by years of war (and not yet reconciled to their governors by the forgetfulness which peace brought). Wilson not only presented the treaty abruptly (actually copies had been procured and unofficially circulated by his political enemies) but he insisted that it be accepted without material change.

Wilson's intransigence was based on his success in incorporating into the treaty the Covenant of the League of Nations. The League, Wilson thought, would preserve the peace and make it possible to remedy the injustices which had crept into the treaty itself. As we know, time proved Wilson's hopes vain; he was not even able to persuade his own country to accept either the treaty or the League. Here we have an individual paradox: the campaign against ratification of the treaty was led by Henry Cabot Lodge, himself long an advocate of organized international action to assure world peace by promoting world order.

As a result of Lodge's parliamentary skill in exploiting partisan opposition and of Wilson's stubbornness (perhaps intensified by the effect of the stroke which felled him in the midst of a speaking campaign intended to win public opinion to support the League of Nations), the Senate refused to ratify the Treaty of Versailles. The United States never did join the League of Nations.

And so far as the United States was concerned, the war to make freedom more nearly universal ended in new restrictions upon individual liberty.

The New Conformity 9

WORLD WAR I IS notable for the number of writers who fought in it and who recorded the war which they had experienced. Other postwar generations may have felt themselves "lost," but the articulate young men who survived this war were probably the first to say that they had been cheated, made to suffer and risk their lives for ends which were not worth sacrifice. Rarely have so many young men in so many countries proclaimed that their leaders had been incompetent in the field, inefficient in the cabinet, and dishonorable at the council table.

Yet, by and large, the old leaders were left in power: communist risings were suppressed in Germany and Hungary; in a number of other countries, Social Democratic parties did assume control of governments, but they could not retain their positions. They lacked the habit of command or, perhaps, it would be more just to say that they trusted that their conservative opponents would acquiesce in their own gradual elimination from power. This the conservatives did not do, and when postwar deflation closed down on the economies of Western Europe, conservative regimes easily replaced the moderate socialists. Yet those conservative regimes could not cope with economic stagnation; in Rostow's terminology, they were unable to transform their countries into economies based on mass sales of durable consumer goods. They in turn lost power, not to socialist revolutionaries as had been feared, but to authoritarian movements which cast off the apparatus of parliamentary government and the rhetoric of democracy and resolved the problem of lagging economic growth by moving men out of the labor market into armies and putting heavy industry to work making arms. The young men who had learned to distrust war went into exile when they were not imprisoned or killed—or when they did not acquiesce.

The United States, however, did succeed in making the economic transition during the 1920's, and its success may have had much to do with the further advance of the new conformity in this country. The strike wave which was discussed in the last chapter was, at least in part, a response to the deflation of the immediate postwar period, when agricultural prices collapsed, war contracts were abruptly terminated, and the labor market was glutted with demobilized soldiers who were flung back into civilian life without any official attempt to ease the transition. The terror with which so many Americans regarded the strikes, and their willingness to accept and participate in repressive measures, was, besides being a response to the Russian Revolution and to the sharp rise [1] in the price of consumer goods which markedly depleted the incomes of many middle-class people, also an expression of continuing hysteria generated by the government's conduct of the war.

For in 1917 and 1918, government propaganda had been whipping Americans to fear and hatred. The unexpectedly

[1] Between 1915 and 1919, prices doubled in the United States, with most of the increase coming in the quarter following March, 1919. See Stanley Coben, *op. cit.*, p. 158.

quick collapse of Germany gave those emotions insufficient opportunity for discharge. Dissent at home, already branded as disloyalty, offered aggression as good a channel as did a foreign enemy. A number of states passed criminal syndicalism acts to cope with I.W.W. activity, as has been mentioned. We have also mentioned the broad range of power which the espionage and sedition laws had given the Federal government. There was thus ample legislative foundation for a movement against civil liberty, and few court decisions raised any dam against the rushing current of suppression. Attacks on free speech in the name of national safety were sanctified by the dictum of Justice Oliver Wendell Holmes, who declared that no right to speak freely would "protect a man in falsely shouting fire in a theater and causing a panic. . . ."[2] Presumably, he thought national enthusiasm for the war so scant, support of the government so tenuous, and social order so genuinely imperiled that forthright criticism of the government's conscription policy constituted a "clear and present danger" to the draft.

By 1920, over 2,000 cases had been brought under the Espionage and Sedition Acts; 239 of those found guilty were still in jail. More than 400 people were committed to military prison for refusing to serve in the Army because they had conscientious objections to war although they were not members of any recognized pacifist religious sect. Conscientious objection was legally respected only if its principles sprang from the tenets of an organized religion to which the objector was formally affiliated.

During 1919 and 1920, after a number of raids on the homes and meeting places of what were regarded as sus-

2 *Schenck* v. *U.S.* 249 U.S. 47 (1918).

picious aliens, some 2,500 formal arrests were made. Some 500 more persons were less formally taken into custody and then released, some after being beaten. More than 500 aliens were sent out of the country under provisions of the immigration laws which allowed the deportation of persons whose presence in the United Staates was considered dangerous to its institutions.[3]

Few members of the "lost generation" protested these violations of liberty nor did they act to "turn the rascals out" by taking part in politics. The most articulate and talented were content to proclaim and even to cultivate their alienation, to mock at their country and to flee from it if they could. By embracing the ethos of alienation, intellectuals contributed to conformity; their mockery of the United States did much to make it unacceptable in intellectual circles to take political questions seriously and so, by a kind of dialectic abstention, they became political conformists.

Their temper is typified in the work of H. L. Mencken, who had not served in the war and who would have scorned to take a direct part in politics. He ferreted out and humorously displayed American social absurdity in all its rich variety. "Dr." Coolidge and "Dr." Wilson were equally objects of his scorn, and most worthy of scorn was the fact that one university had let Wilson earn a doctorate and others had been willing to confer an honorary degree on

[3] *Deportations Delirium of 1920* (Chicago: Charles H. Kerr & Co., 1923). The author, Louis Post, was Assistant Secretary of Labor and able to moderate the impact of the panicked drive against aliens with "dangerous thoughts" launched by the Attorney General and his new Federal Bureau of Investigation. The 1920 raids against leftist-oriented aliens were motivated by desire to find those responsible for the mailing of about forty bombs to important politicians and businessmen; none of the guilty was ever caught.

the non-intellectual Coolidge. The businessman, in Mencken's opinion, might be ridiculous or even thievish, but the political reformer was contemptible because he was probably a sour puritan as well as a hopeful fool.

Meanwhile, the new conformity was developing rapidly, offsetting the revolt of the alienated young intellectuals. They railed at the *booboisie*, to use Mencken's word, saying these fellows should not interfere with the doings and diversions of their betters. But the intellectuals' opposition was merely verbal and was ineffectual.

Change, it has often been observed, is frightening, and many men cling to an accustomed manner of life even when that life is miserable. In the United States, where change was a norm, World War I made its pace swifter than ever. To cite one instance: in 1914 Americans owed the rest of the world about $3.68 billion; in 1919, the rest of the world owed Americans $2.9 billion, a sum which rose to more than $6 billion in 1924. An economic posture had probably not changed so radically since the Conquistadors brought Spain the accumulated silver and gold of the Aztec and the Inca, and even that change had proceeded at a somewhat slower rate. Of course, as we have shown, technological and economic change had been moving cumulatively, ever since England began exporting at least some phases of the Industrial Revolution to this country. We have seen, too, how successfully the political leaders of the post-Civil War period, fearing change, evaded meeting the new problems of an industrial nation. We have noted, further, that the progressive movement, however ineptly, tried to deal with some of the issues which change had generated.

By the early twenties, it was more evident than ever that directing change implied further change. A significant num-

ber of Americans tried to avoid the pain which change implied. Many had already been uprooted, shifting their
lives from farm and small town to cities; many others feared
uprooting. And a decisive number of Americans carried
their old ways of responding into their new environment.
Thus, they sought to preserve the familiar ethnic make-up
of the nation and to check the cities, or at least to harass
certain kinds of behavior which were more common in
cities.

Let us first consider the problem of immigration. Nativism has roots in the American past, going back to the
1830's at least, when Irish Catholic immigrants were physically attacked, economically discriminated against (even
though their labor was needed and welcome), and described
as makers of slums and breeders of criminals. As each new
group of immigrants arrived, it met similar treatment, but
although organized groups of Americans did advocate
formal discrimination against immigrants—restriction on
naturalization and the right to vote particularly—restriction
of immigration itself had few supporters until the 1880's.[4]
Then organized labor demanded that Chinese workers be
forbidden to enter the United States and succeeded in
having that demand enacted into law. Not until the 1890's,
however, did spokesmen for the "better element," such as
Henry Cabot Lodge, join labor in seeking to restrict immigration. Lodge and some of those who worked with him
may have been aware of the pressure on wages which
roused their constituents' resentment, but they tended to

---

[4] Among the supporters of restriction was Seth Luther, an eccentric
partisan of the Lowell millgirl and her right to a living wage. As early as
the 1830's, Luther argued that if manufacturers were entitled to tariff
protection against competition from foreign goods, workers were en-
tiitled to protection against competition from foreign laborers.

talk about the nation's Anglo-Saxon heritage and the danger of its being submerged by incoming Slavs, Italians, and Jews, with their alien religions, their unfashionable foreign tongues, and their possible susceptibility to socialist ideas.

The presence of large numbers of "unassimilated" foreigners had roused fears during the war among these who remembered that there were 14 million foreign-born persons in the country and about the same number whose parents were foreign-born. When peace came, and large-scale immigration resumed, traditional nativist anxiety finally overbore desire for a continuing supply of cheap labor. Congress limited the number of immigrants in 1921; it assigned to each European nation represented in the American population a quota of 3 per cent of its nationals living in the country in 1910. The base year was shifted to 1890 in 1924, in order to shut out more southern and eastern Europeans, and the quota reduced to 2 per cent; the total number of immigrants permitted to enter was also limited.[5]

The immigration acts of the 1920's (and by and large they are the law today) are symptomatic of a desire to have Americans as like each other as possible. Without recruits from abroad, what had been a distinctive, though limited, immigrant cultural life dwindled away: foreign-language theaters all but disappeared and the foreign-language press lost circulation.[6] The 1960's talk about cultural pluralism

[5] All Asian and African immigration was barred; Western Hemisphere migration was left unrestricted. The law went into force just as the Depression struck; during the 1930's, more migrants left the United States than entered. In 1952 Congress revised the immigration law, repealed the provisions excluding Asians, and assigned small quotas to Asian countries. The principle of restriction remained unaffected, however, and exclusion for ideological reasons, which had begun in 1903 when anarchists were barred, continued.

[6] This situation has changed somewhat with the continuing entry of Spanish-speaking persons from Puerto Rico who, as American citizens, cannot be excluded.

and the immigrant heritage, but what actually survives, except for the habit of ethnic voting, is what some Jewish essayists call *kitchen culture*—difference of custom rather than an infusion of creativity.[7]

Since immigrants had tended to move toward the cities after 1870 and since cities were the evidence of that social and economic change which on the farm and in the small town generated fear for an accustomed way of life, it is easy to understand rural support for laws limiting immigration; immigration increased the population of cities and might, ultimately, increase their relative political power within the states. Rural legislators, state and Federal, supported a number of measures that tried to exact uniformity of behavior and conformity to the mores of an older and presumably a better world.

The moral superiority of country folk to city people is a cliché at least as old as Aristophanes, whose farmers and squires speak for peace, common sense, and piety, condemning the demagogues, philosophers, and artists, the Cleons and Euripides and Socrates who infested Athens and lured men into voting for war, applauding iconoclastic poetry, and losing respect for the faith of their fathers. So far as the United States is concerned, Thomas Jefferson, as urbane a man as ever praised rural simplicity, may be taken as the most noteworthy spokesman for the belief that political as well as moral virtue resides in the country.

[7] In one respect, whatever our contemporary verbal commitment to cultural pluralism, America today is far less pluralistic than European nations, nearly all of which give tax support to religious schools. In the United States, tax-supported schools continue to function as a means of blurring cultural distinctions and assimilating divergence. The development of Catholic school systems, and the recent growth of parochial education among other religious groups, may point toward a radical change in this respect.

Jefferson's contention continues to be heard in our time, although the land now supports only a small part of the nation's people and rural areas exert a political influence wholly disproportionate to their population, their wealth—or their representatives' demonstrated capacity for statesmanship.

We have already said that the farmers' economic objectives were defeated when, in 1896, Bryan and free silver failed to win the presidential election. Farm representatives had no greater success in the 1920's when, shifting from support of monetary inflation, they tried to maintain the prices of agricultural staples by securing the equivalent of the Federal subsidies we now have. Twice, such measures were adopted by Congress, but they were defeated by presidential veto.

Rural influence had more weight in other respects. Current studies of the election of 1924 seem to show that Al Smith owed his defeat less to his religion than to his being a representative of urban ways, particularly of the cities' persistence in refusal to give even lip service to Prohibition.

To persons who live in a situation where fear lest man will not survive is no mere fantasy, it seems strange indeed that American governments, state and Federal, should have spent effort and money in an attempt to keep people from drinking. Prohibition has been seen as a response to the industrialist's need for a sober work force, as an expression of middle-class reformers' desire to end the political influence of the local saloon, as a testimony to the exasperation of women who saw their husbands spending on drink the money that should feed their families. But Prohibition is also an instance of the new conformity, in that it was an attempt to make everyone accept a manner of life which some found to be good.

Again, like political nativism, Prohibition has roots in the nineteenth century. At first, those who felt that Americans drank too much—and at the turn of the nineteenth century no group activity, from a barn raising to a minister's ordination, could proceed without notable consumption of rum—tried only to persuade. "Washingtonian Societies," bringing to the cause an aura of patriotism from the first President's name, were organized, with their membership pledged to drink only in *moderation*. Later, Blue Ribbon Bands of children promised *never* to drink. Women, who seem to have left the joys of drink to their men, urged their suitors to avoid the "social glass." In the 1840's, and particularly in the 1850's, persuasion was reinforced by state laws; often these allowed the sale of liquor only by the gallon, apparently on the theory that a man would drink less at home than in a sociable barroom. These laws were not effective, and enthusiasm for Prohibition soon diminished.

The movement revived after the 1870's, and it was more successful, especially after the Anti-Saloon League was organized and grew into one of the nation's most effective pressure groups. By 1914 eleven states, mostly in the rural South and West, adopted prohibitory laws; others permitted localities to forbid the sale of liquor within their bounds. Congress cooperated by forbidding the shipment of liquor from wet states into those which were dry. The movement gathered momentum: by 1918, thirty-seven states were officially dry and wartime demand for conserving grain gave Congress reason to ban the distillation of whiskey, a measure passed over Wilson's veto, incidentally. Congress then offered the nation a Constitutional amendment allowing Federal regulation of the manufacture, sale, and transportation of intoxicating liquor. The necessary number of states ratified the amendment, and the United States became a dry nation.

For a decade after Congress passed the Volstead Act (which defined an intoxicant as a beverage having an alcoholic content greater than ½ of 1 per cent) what seems like a disproportionate amount of attention was given to Prohibition. The situation is somewhat easier to understand when one sees it in terms of a characteristic middle-class desire to improve one's neighbor by making him more like oneself. The urban world fought back—although Prohibition did have support in the cities, one may reasonably conjecture that some of the city Drys were people of farm or small-town origin. Spokesmen for the alienated intellectuals—here again Mencken is noteworthy—used Prohibition as evidence to support their conviction that reformers were fools and hypocrites and that, except as a source of amusement, American politics was unworthy of the attention of any civilized man. Because Al Smith was a forthright Wet, Mencken thought he had some claim on the Presidency. Because Herbert Hoover saw merit in the Prohibition laws, he was unworthy of the office to which he certainly would be elected in 1928. (Hoover was also shallow, self-seeking, and without honor, but that would not prevent him or any man from being elected President, Mencken thought.[8])

Some states, notably New York, refused to help the Federal government enforce the law. By the 1930's it had become evident that Prohibition, which was intended to free

[8] H. L. Mencken, *On Politics*, ed. by Malcolm Moos (New York: Vintage Books, 1960), pp. 209-16.

American life of a corrupting influence, was actually encouraging the spread of corruption: respectable people preferred breaking the law to forgoing their liquor; their demands were met by smuggling and illegal manufacture, both accompanied by gang violence; the venality of those who enforced the law came to be taken for granted, and the "racket" took its place among the forms of American business enterprise. Repeal of the Eighteenth Amendment did not purge the body politic of corruption, but it did free the Federal government of obligation to enforce what was evidently an unenforceable law. In this respect, at least, the American public almost consistently refused to conform.

A third and at least nominally more successful attempt to impose conformity by law is to be seen in the adoption of statutes which forbade teaching the theory of evolution in tax-supported schools. Tennessee is the best-known instance of a state which adopted such a law, but Tennessee was not alone. Similar measures were introduced in a number of states and adopted in Arkansas, Mississippi, and Texas. Florida's legislature, in response to appeals by Bryan, adopted a resolution condemning the teaching of evolution, and for a number of years, California's state textbook commission accomplished the same purpose by refusing to buy texts which presented evolution as an accepted part of scientific knowledge. Generally, enthusiasm for anti-evolution laws was greatest among rural legislators, for they were most likely to be Scriptural literalists themselves and to feel threatened by the increasing influence of more modern ideas. One can understand their wish to guard young people against the effect of such disturbing theories as evolution, which denied the literal truth of the Bible and seemed to assimilate men to the beasts and thus to excuse immoral behavior. Parents of secondary-school children showed little concern for the adoption of the new laws—and that was taken as further evidence of the wickedness of the city, where parents did not care whether their children were protected from false teaching or not (attendance at high school was more common in town than country as late as the mid-twenties, in spite of the growing use of bus transportation to take rural youngsters to school).

The constitutionality of the Tennessee anti-evolution statute was never fully tested, despite the notorious Scopes trial—the Tennessee case in which a young science teacher presented the forbidden material to his class so that he could be charged with breaking the law, tried, and, by appealing, have the statute subjected to judicial review. Clarence Darrow, celebrated as a defender of forlorn hopes—political radicals particularly—was Scopes' attorney; Scopes' conviction was a foregone conclusion [9] and the trial turned into a circus; Darrow baited the aging William Jennings Bryan, who appeared as a friend of the court in support of the law, but, although the trial was reported at length and much discussed, little attention seems to have been paid to what now appears the major issue: how much control over the content of public education may be legitimately exercised by representatives of the taxpayers who meet its cost.

In the preceding discussion of some aspects of the new conformity, we have noted that nativism, Prohibition, and even legal attempts to check the spread of dangerous

[9] It proved impossible to carry an appeal to the Supreme Court. Scopes was fined $100. The highest Tennessee court affirmed the constitutionality of the anti-evolution statute. It overruled the judgment against Scopes, however; the lower court had no authority to levy a fine greater than $50; hence it had exceeded its authority in punishing Scopes. Because the lower court's verdict was thus overruled, the defendant, Scopes, had no grounds for appeal.

thoughts had a long background in America. But the new conformity had other facets. The two most characteristic are private law enforcement, also a deeply rooted American social habit, and the cumulative pressure which technological development was exerting toward uniformity. (We discuss the second point first.)

By its very nature, industrialization imposes uniformity: it exacts a uniform discipline from workers; it offers consumers uniform goods. If this push toward uniformity had been evident in nineteenth-century America—and it was, reinforced perhaps by the constant movement of settlement which tended to break up local differences—it grew stronger after World War I, when the automobile, the film, and radio broadcasting simultaneously became important in American life.

The automobile is a standardized product, manufactured under standardized conditions, and employed in ways that tend to standardize men's pattern of life and to make man's imprint on the land more uniform. Here, too, the phenomenon is not wholly novel. The foreign traveler, unaware of American nuances, had long found it hard to tell one Middle Western town from another. In his *American Commonwealth*, James Bryce had noted how much alike the smaller American cities of the 1880's were, with almost identical main streets lined by laundries operated by pigtailed Chinese, by ice cream parlors, barber shops, hotels, undertakers' shops, and, if the community were large enough, those streets were striped by horse-car lines.

As automobiles became cheaper, more were sold and Americans demanded and got better roads to drive them on. In the 1920's a day's trip was no longer limited to the number of miles a horse could be safely driven. The farmer was somewhat emancipated from the railroad and the local merchant. He could trade at a distance, getting new goods almost as soon as city people. The "rube" could no longer be easily distinguished by his clothes (neither, for that matter, could the laborer); his distinctive turns of speech, too, were being changed.

In respect of manners, appearance, and speech, radio broadcasting and the film increased pressures toward uniformity. The automobile brought people into closer physical proximity; broadcasting and moving pictures exposed men's desires and emotions to the same stimuli. Radio advertising sought to create a market for identical goods, and whatever its claims, commercial broadcasting exists in order to sell advertising. One may, of course, doubt whether people become essentially more alike because they respond to encouragement to wash with the identical soap, smoke the identical cigarette, drink the identical soft drink, watch the same stereotyped entertainment. (Perhaps they are willing to accept identical goods because they are themselves so much alike.)

Exposure to standardized entertainment has a feedback effect. Since the producers of such entertainment are engaged in a commercial enterprise, often focused on selling particular commodities, they need very large audiences in order to earn profits. They seek to find a common denominator of taste, accordingly, and to purvey what that taste seems to want. The more successful the purveyor, the more vulgar the denominator has tended to become. And the more vulgar and standardized the denominator, the greater the incentive to vulgarize it further.

Since the 1920's, Americans by the million have simultaneously exposed themselves to the same fantasies, whether on the moving picture screen or the TV tube which has so largely replaced it. By the million, they have listened to the same songs, laughed at the same jokes, and, with the advent of political broadcasting, kindled to the same political slogans—or come to regard the political speeches and conventions which were brought into their homes as part of the same manufactured spectacle by which they are persuaded to buy goods. Possible blurring of the line between fantasy and actuality, because they are heard and seen on the same instruments which present them with the same kind of immediacy, is not among our concerns here, although the social psychologist might well give the possibility some thought. Here we raise the question of whether commercial entertainment that presents fictional gratification of fantasies which its makers presume to exist among audiences may not create an even broader prevalence of such fantasy, and a greater uniformity in the form which fantasy may take in men's minds.

The technological developments of the 1920's made mass consumption of mass-produced goods ever more necessary if the economy were to flourish. And in order to have mass consumption, it was necessary to have uniformity of taste. Here again, feedback effects occur; the more uniform the goods available, the more uniform tastes tend to become. On this level, the push toward uniformity of behavior required no formal coercion. One might, to be sure, mention in passing the issue of film censorship. Since motion pictures were seen by so many young people, it seemed appropriate to protect the purity of their minds by forbidding material which would incite to crime or provide too high a level of sexual excitement. Early attempts to have the film share in the constitutional protection of freedom of speech failed, when in 1915 the Supreme Court said: ". . . the exhibition of moving pictures is a business, pure and simple, conducted for profit like other spectacles, not to be regarded by the Ohio Constitution [the case came from Ohio on appeal], we think, as part of the press of the country or as organs of public opinion." [10]

State boards of film censorship multiplied thereafter, and their decisions and personnel roused the amusement—and the wrath—of those who disagreed with the Supreme Court and thought that the moving picture might be an art even if its exhibition was a business.[11] Quite as ludicrous as the criteria used by official censors were the standards of taste formally established for itself by the film industry in what was generally known as the Hays code.[12] That code was obeyed for many years, and provided that films be designed to offend nobody, neither the sexually conservative, the members of any acceptable political party, nor the religious sensibilities of any group with votes. Consequently, the code did all that formal rules could do to make certain that no American film dealt with any subject that could interest a cultivated adult in any fashion that such an adult could respect. The Hollywood film did not lose money on that

[10] *Mutual Film Corp.* v. *Ohio Industrial Commission,* 236 U.S. 230 (1915), cited in Milton R. Konvitz, *Bill of Rights Reader* (Ithaca, N.Y.: Cornell University Press, 1954), pp. 414-19. The 1915 decision was overruled in *Burstyn, Inc.* v. *Wilson,* 343 U.S. 495 (1952), which extended the protection of the First and Fourteenth Amendments to moving pictures. The 1952 decision did not forbid censorship; it merely insisted that the statute on which the censorship was based be clear and definite in its definition of objectionable material.

[11] For pictures and listings of censored material, *see* M. L. Ernst and Pare Lorentz, *Censored: the Private Life of the Movie* (New York: Cape and Smith, 1930).

[12] Will Hays had been Postmaster General and dispenser of patronage in the Harding administration and, for that reason, was considered politically useful and therefore peculiarly fit to make certain that motion pictures were morally inoffensive.

account. It had found the way to appeal to a universal desire for passive gratification; American moving pictures
were as popular in foreign theaters as filmed American TV
shows are today in foreign homes. One might say, therefore, that Americans were first and most nakedly exposed
to a diet of uniform entertainment, but they are not unique
in their willingness to accept it, to follow the fads it might
generate, and to mold their fantasies and their purchases as
it suggests.

Pressures for conformity coming from the law, and from
an economy shifting its orientation from demand for thrift
and production to a new demand for the use of credit in
order to increase consumption, were not the only factors
making for uniformity in American life. The anxiety generated by awareness of change gave rise to overt, although
extra-legal pressure for conformity of behavior. Again,
such pressure is not wholly novel in America. Tar and
feathers were employed as an instrument of persuasion in
the Revolutionary period. The defects of formal law enforcement were made good by "Judge Lynch" long before
the Vigilantes took over in the California of the early 1850's.
If Americans are a lawless people, they are often most lawless when they join together to enforce what they think
ought to be the law.

Such independent organization of public-spirited persons
had been encouraged during the war. The American Protective League was formally disbanded in 1919-20, but its
spirit lingered on.[13] Unofficial aid to law enforcement was
continued, most notoriously by the Ku Klux Klan. The
Klan had its origin in the South, but it achieved great success in rural areas and small towns of the Middle West. A

[13] Coben, *op. cit.*, p. 199.

shocking episode involving the sexual abuse and subsequent death of a young woman—in which an Indiana Klan official was found guilty of murder—did much to end the Klan's political power.[14] Its acts, its organization, and its targets, however, further clarify the animus behind some of the laws which have been discussed earlier. Nor should we ignore the role in the Klan's growth that was played by a professional public relations man and promoter who saw the money-making possibilities of an organization which met in costume and delighted in ornamenting its regalia.[15]

The Klan professed to defend the purity of womanhood, the integrity of America's Anglo-Saxon heritage, the dominance of the white race, and the position of the Protestant religion. Masked in pointed white hoods and white robes, Klansmen raided, whipping labor organizers, bootleggers, and prostitutes, warning young people not to park and pet, burning fiery crosses, smashing the windows of stores owned by Jews, denouncing the Pope, and uncostumed, dictating the nomination of state officials. The Klan's strength lay outside the cities, as has been said; from the cities came the alien groups and ideas it feared. In the upsurge of the Klan, therefore, many historians see evidence of a forward thrust of rural America against the swiftly altering postwar world.

The Klan was not the only organization which Americans joined; indeed, one can see in the Klan, where men found fellowship in hate, a degenerate form of the fraternal orders into which Americans had been flocking since the mid-nineteenth century. "Joining" had long been consid-

[14] Arnold S. Rice, *Ku Klux Klan in American Politics* (Washington, D.C.: Public Affairs Press, 1962), pp. 12, 131.

[15] Ibid., p. 7.

ered a distinctively American practice. De Tocqueville had
talked of how readily Americans set up associations for
every conceivable purpose, from making money to spread-
ing appreciation of the fine arts by selling lottery tickets on
new American paintings; and he had pointed out how alien
such freedom of association was to European society, where
governments were jealous of any secular tie other than that
which bound subject and sovereign, citizen and state. By
the 1920's, "joining" had become so prevalent that some
Americans began to be aware of its significance. Again, it
was novelists like Sinclair Lewis who showed the Middle
Western businessman in the throes of fraternity.

Conformity offered great rewards in the twenties. Conformity to the image of the "regular guy," the effective
salesman, would bring a young man economic success. Conformity to the demands of strong local groups—the Klan
and the Anti-Saloon League developed the art of exerting
pressure against candidates to an extraordinary degree—
could bring a man political success. Social success, too, came
to the conventional. Americans have never cherished ec-
centricity, as the English are reputed to do, but in the 1920's
what seemed like increasing numbers of Americans began to
voice their discomfort loudly in its suspected presence.

The American artist and intellectual, as has been said,
protested against the new conformity, largely by developing a conformity of his own. And in this conformity, alienation generated a new kind of community.

In earlier chapters, we have pointed out how the needs
of a society constantly thrusting into new territory created
patterns of life which had small space for the sensitive man,
for the disinterested scholar, or for the artist whose creativity could not shape itself into the mutual daydreaming

of the popular novel. Such people were relatively few, and very lonely. The roll of neglected genius is easy to call, from Poe and Melville through Stephen Crane. It is possible, though perhaps a little less easy, to hear the artists' counter-rejection. Even Mark Twain, popular though he was, added "The Man Who Corrupted Hadleyburg" to his unflattering description of conventional good people.

Yet not until after World War I do large numbers of talented writers call the American community enemy, rather than regrettably purblind companion. Novelists like Sinclair Lewis [16] show the community as a brake upon creative effort, whether that is absurd and groping, as was Carol Kennicott's in *Main Street*, or farsighted and wise, as was Arrowsmith's. In *Babbitt* Lewis shows the smothering effect of the community even on the man who accepts it, the conformist, realtor by occupation, who is wakened by the trademarked alarm clock, rises from his standard mattress to brush his teeth with his brand-name toothpaste, eats his well-advertised breakfast food, and so through the rest of his ordered day.

The theory that the mores operate to stifle creativity is a romantic convention, to be sure, but the nineteenth-century romantic still felt betrayed: the community should have a place for him; his fellows should at least try to appreciate what he was doing. The rebellious artist of the 1920's trans-

[16] Low though Lewis' literary reputation has fallen, there can be small question of his astuteness as an observer of the American scene. A generation after he created Babbitt, sociologists began making reputations by recording that character's existence and trying to explore the psychological causes of his behavior. In his reports of Rotary meetings and the like, Lewis shows what the professional student of society was not to report for another decade at least, the attempt of men who had met the requirements for success in a standardizing world to secure recognition of themselves as persons.

formed his alienation into a shield behind which he could
work to express himself.

Generally, both the artist and the educated man who
accepted the new version of the romantic convention knew
the self he expressed; one does not find many novels of the
period in which the protagonist is in search of a self. Rather,
the protagonist searches for an environment that will allow
the self to develop. Even if that self must be "found," the
search is a matter of finding a man's true work and so establishing his place in the world. The self exists; the hero
(or heroine) whom it inhabits never questions its presence
or its integrity.

Among the more conventional, meanwhile, the American folk hero took on a new shape; the self-made man in the
1920's was a salesman [17] rather than an industrialist; and
"selling yourself" became a term of commendation. The
salesman still had a self, however; the peculiar corroding
doubt of our day had not yet affected a people who were
aware of no experience except the experience of success.

Women and children, too, were influenced by the slogan
of self-expression during the 1920's. For self-expression became a watchword used by rebellious young people, emancipated women, educators, and, of course, artists and
intellectuals, actual and aspiring. Educators, inspired by the
ideas of John Dewey and some versions of the insights of
Freud, began urging parents to create a family environment
which would accept a child's instincts while it taught him
to govern their expression. This attitude contrasted sharply
with traditional ideas about child nature, whether those
derived from the sinful-little-demon or small-angel theory,

[17] Bruce Barton, head of an important advertising agency, discovered
the *Man Nobody Knows* to be Christ the salesman.

and like all new viewpoints, this tended to be distorted in its application. Many people, learning about the new attitude at second hand, accepted complete permissiveness as the proper method of child rearing, a misinterpretation whose consequences continue to affect many lives.

In certain respects, middle-class women had long been considered peculiarly free and fortunate in America. Henry James had indeed pitied them because they were so superior to their husbands, who led limited, money-grubbing lives, but he did not challenge the assumption that women ought to be superior, however they might suffer for it. Now in the 1920's, women began asserting a right to express and to fulfill themselves. Their emancipation took on a new cast: a generation earlier, they had claimed rights; they had demanded the vote for example—in part because they had been set upon a pedestal. If women were morally superior to men, as everyone acknowledged, their virtues should be effective beyond the range of their cook stoves and their parlors. In the 1920's, middle-class women stepped down; the hand that rocked the cradle might still rule the world, but the foot had come off the pedestal and onto the rail of a speakeasy bar. Women were claiming their right to enjoy themselves in ways hitherto reserved for men. In the 1920's, too, partly as a result of the war's demand for workers, middle-class women began to take it for granted that they would work for their living. They aspired to "careers"; they took jobs; a substantial number of them pursued job or career even after marriage. In the arts, women continued to produce distinguished work, of course, but women have been artists since Sappho was acclaimed in Greece as *the* poetess; it was middle-class women's assertion of a right to express themselves and to enjoy an equal place in the workaday world which was novel.

The political preoccupations and much of the intellectual excitement of the 1920's, in succeeding decades came to seem puerile. The 1930's faced a depression; the 1940's had a war to fight. But to some looking back from the 1960's, and particularly to those who saw the years after World War II as a bland wasteland, the brashness of the twenties seems confidence, its puerility endearingly naïve, and its very corruption innocence.

The Interchangeable Man   10

THUS FAR WE HAVE only hinted at what was felt to be the extraordinary economic situation of the United States in the 1920's when, to use Rostow's formulation again, the United States entered into the period characterized by mass consumption of the durable-goods output of mass production. We have mentioned the rather brief postwar depression and the burst of strikes and counterviolence which accompanied that. We have hinted, too, at the declining position of agriculture, where the production of staples was sharply affected by the changing of fashion at home and the shrinking of markets abroad. Not many spokesmen for agriculture talked much about the effect of the new nationalism on international trade and the demand for American wheat and cotton. Fewer still seemed much aware that the American woman had changed shape; no girl wanted to be plump any more and few were willing to wear cotton. But as staple prices fell, output rose, and Congress resounded with the protests and the remedial plans of insurgent Western representatives.

As has been mentioned, the insurgents' plans for government support of farm prices either failed to pass or were aborted by presidential veto. Farm income continued to fall; the burden of debt grew heavier. Ignored, other weak areas in the economy grew weaker: the market for soft coal shrank; the cotton textile industry moved into low-wage areas and still was affected by competition from lower-cost countries; the railroads paid for past financial offenses by top-heavy debt structures which hampered the roads in meeting competition from the automobile. Signals warning of weakening in the economy appeared and were disregarded, for it was considered impolitic to have the Federal Reserve System raise interest rates in 1927, shortly before a presidential election. Furthermore, respected economists like Professor Thomas Carver of Harvard said that old-fashioned economic crises would no longer occur. The United States had experienced a wholly peaceful revolution and entered a new economic era in which standards of living might be expected to rise continuously.

Carver was correct in one detail: the collapse of 1929 was so large in its scale and so broad in its impact that it might well be accounted something new under the economic sun. And it was received in a new way. During the years of prosperity, leaders of the American business community had claimed and been given honor for what they had wrought. The depression was indeed caused by the operation of impersonal economic factors at home and abroad, as the business leaders protested, but many Americans thought those who accepted praise should not now refuse blame. General confidence in business leadership was at least somewhat depleted.

Depleted too was the ideal of individual endeavor and particularly of individual thrift. With not only the collapse of speculation but the failure of many banks, carrying with them the life savings of the thrifty, caution in regard to money seemed futile. In regard to spending, pressure toward mortgaging the future had grown during the twenties. Installment buying, which had not been considered entirely suitable for middle-class families (except for acquiring houses and pianos), became respectable and necessary as more and more people bought automobiles for no other purpose than the pleasure of having and using them. The first steps along the road toward life by credit card had been taken, although the device itself was not yet invented. Conviction that stock prices would continue to rise had infected increasing numbers of people so thoroughly that they were willing to borrow in order to speculate, a practice which heretofore had usually been limited to the professional market operator.

In regard to saving, a banking system which was by no means closely, efficiently, or centrally supervised had long made rates of bank failure in America uncommonly high for a country of its wealth and state of development. (Of the banks operating in 1920, 29 per cent failed between 1922 and 1931.) With the collapse of the stock market came a parallel collapse of the banking system. When bank after large bank failed, the Federal government came to the rescue in 1932: the Hoover administration set up a huge corporation which lent money to big institutions on the premise that they would support the position of smaller banks.

That hope was not fulfilled because the large banks, after they had consolidated their own positions, had little left of the Federal funds they had been allowed to borrow. The banking system continued to deteriorate. Farm prices continued to fall despite reluctant government efforts to maintain them through purchases of the Commodity Credit Corporation. Employment shrank; wages fell; working conditions deteriorated; community resources for preventing starvation dwindled. Yet the Republican leadership continued to argue that the depression would end of itself through the "enlightened self-interest" of individuals and that government must not interfere. Or, if it did, its interference should be as limited as possible and funneled through such enterprises as large banks, railroads, and other business organizations. This position has its supporters still, supporters convinced that their view is morally valid as well as practically successful. Government interference during the 1930's prolonged the depression, they claim, and demoralized individuals.

In the early 1930's, however, the electorate was ready to take what the opposition considered the morally invalid road; the foundations of the economy had been undermined. Abroad, meanwhile, the pillars of the economic structure were pulled down: Britain went off the gold standard. Only people taught that there was no legitimate currency but one based on gold and that Britain was the prophet of that currency can appreciate the shock of learning that Britain had been forced to abjure the creed. Perhaps these economic shocks were most damaging to the framework within which the basic American social premises had operated, though the disintegration of the Versailles settlement and the dissolution of international order also brought shock after numbing shock to those who lived through the 30's.

During earlier depressions, it had not seemed unreasonable to advise the jobless to leave the cities and return to the farms. But now a commercialized agriculture, itself operating at a loss, could not profitably absorb the unemployed. Few farmers were fully self-subsisting; farming might not be an efficiently operated business, but it was tied to the market as closely as any manufacturing enterprise and rather less able to cut cost and output at need. Subsistence farming did have its advocates, to be sure. People like Andrew Lytle [1] urged farmers—especially Southern farmers—to secede from the money economy, give up their gasoline engines, grow their own food, make their own tools, provide their own entertainment, and so tell the unrewarding twentieth century to go to hell. But most farmers, Southern as well as Middle Western, preferred to sign up for Federal price-support programs under the new Agricultural Adjustment Administration created by the Roosevelt administration when the Democrats were returned to power in 1932; farmers concluded that only governmentally directed action could compel systematic reduction of output and bring higher prices in consequence.

Without alternatives, unemployed workers in cities felt themselves caught in a world which had no use for them. Since no one wanted to buy what they could make, employers could not be expected to keep them at work. The situation was difficult enough in metropolitan centers where a variety of industries existed. But many plants had left the cities, moving closer to raw materials, to electric power, to people willing to work for less money. Such plants were often the sole source of wages in a community. When they operated on short time or shut down entirely, no other work was available. In many instances, therefore, the initiative and industry in which men were told to and did put their faith were all but palpably irrelevant.

A generation has passed since the 1930's. Memory of the

---

[1] Lytle has produced novels, essays, a biography of Nathan Bedford Forrest, and a number of short stories.

collapse has receded. Historians and economists build reputations in disputing the wisdom of the policies taken for dealing with the depression. Certainly, the New Deal program did not push the economy back into an upward spiral. But countries which followed more classically oriented lines of policy were scarcely more successful in returning to peacetime prosperity. That which had gone down gave little sign of moving upward of itself: slight advances in the application of technology gave no impetus toward an upward movement of the business cycle, nor were there unexpected discoveries of gold to affect price levels. Indeed, exhausted inventories were replenished by fewer workers. Such American economists as Alvin Hansen said that the classical, market-governed economy had come to the end of its rope; only governmental intervention could keep productivity from strangling itself.[2]

The rulers of Germany, Italy, and Japan acclaimed war meanwhile and their people applauded: preparing for war seemed better than stagnation. In 1936, both as an economic measure and because the danger of war was becoming obvious, the United States, too, began a massive program of rearmament. Congress voted $911 million, and many of those who feared the consequences of governmental taxing and spending in order to keep people alive were not afraid of spending and taxing in order to prepare for killing possible enemies.

The enemies were real enough and the American rearmament program which followed 1937 proved necessary. It did little to assist economic growth, however; it did not drain the pool of unemployment. Even the somewhat dis-

---

[2] Alvin Hansen, *Fiscal Policy and Business Cycles* (New York: W. W. Norton, 1941).

appointing recovery which occurred with the renewal of foreign demand after war broke out in 1939 did not cope with depression's glut of things and people.[3] Only American entry into the war did that.

In modern war, the relevance of the action of individuals is more unpredictable than in older patterns of warfare; nevertheless, in action the utmost strain of effort is necessary if the individual is to protect himself. The mechanization of warfare added a new dimension to men's sense of being caught in some great movement of nature when they were involved in war. This is not new; *War and Peace* is only the most striking example of the view that history moves by laws of its own and that, in contrast to the events in which they have their being, rulers and "little people" are alike insignificant.

World War I had brought the machine age into military life, introducing the use of machine guns, tanks, submarines, the airplane and dirigible. Men carried their destructiveness into what had once been the untroubled air and the secluded depths of the sea. But the full meaning of what had occurred was not clear until the 1940's, for only then did commanders make conscious use of the new weapons to strike at what has long been known to be the basic military objective, the enemy's will to fight and his capacity to produce the materials needed for fighting. The civilian was exposed as he had not been, perhaps, since the Thirty Years' War, and he was threatened not by individuals or bands of marauders, but from the air. The bombed civilian could do little to protect himself. Yet in destroyed cities, in devastated countrysides, in the midst of persecutions, individuals exploited

[3] Since the Neutrality Acts of 1934 and 1937 had all but forbidden the sale of supplies and war materials on credit, foreign orders may have been smaller than would have otherwise been expected.

the unforeseen, and by ingenuity, or the lucky chance of a hiding place and food, kept themselves and others alive.

This pattern of experience was not relevant to the United States. Although off Alaska and in the Pacific, American soil was occupied by a foreign enemy, no American city was bombed, and the only mainland Americans uprooted because of the war were those of Japanese descent who were herded into concentration camps. But Americans, too, were seized by tension, caught between a dim sense of responsibility and a rather sharp awareness that the situation was not merely beyond the ordinary person's comprehension but probably beyond the grasp of those whom he trusted to direct it. World War I had produced few heroes to be worshipped; the only one of its generals to win high office did not get beyond Vice-President. If Charles G. Dawes is remembered at all by people who are not concerned with the problem of German reparations payments in the 1920's, it is as Hell 'n Maria Dawes who smoked an extraordinary kind of pipe. World War II produced the anti-hero, the sad sack and the griper, or, more accurately, the people who described the war made the anti-hero an image which the common reader was ready to accept. And although the chief American military commander of World War II did become President in 1952, Dwight Eisenhower was not presented to the electorate as a hero. Those unkindly disposed toward contemporary methods of influencing opinion would say that he had been marketed as an image of paternity, virtuous and blandly vague, like the good father of the mass media.

As change and war left many Americans both frustrated and weary in 1919, so war and depression-born change left Americans tired and frustrated after 1946. In both periods, many sought and even found comfort in search of, and attack on, villains. In both instances, too, communism provided the most visible symbol of challenge to the values of laissez-faire. By the 1950's, moreover, the Soviet Union had become genuinely competitive, militarily and politically. For the first time within the experience of those who showed themselves most intensely concerned, it became conceivable that this country might not always, and without too much exertion, be top dog.[4]

The resurgence of conservatism was later in coming than it had been after the First World War, but Americans responded in rather similar ways. Politicians built careers on ferreting out subversives. New laws limited Americans in the exercise of freedom to organize and make their political opinions known. The political career of Joseph McCarthy had probably terminated before his death, but the political technique he had used so skillfully is still, to a degree, being employed. And for a decade at least, Americans felt the impact of a drive to purify government and industry (now often in the service of the military) of people who thought dangerous thoughts. A new and effective impetus was given long-standing trends toward privatism, alienation, and conformity. At the same time, observers and pollsters reported certain changes in Americans' proclaimed attitudes toward individual economic achievement.

Ours seems to be the age of the questionnaire. Sociologists, psychologists, political scientists, and industrial market

[4] In the 1960's, economic defeat at least seems more likely to come from friends than enemies. A resurgent Atlantic Europe, building upon initial United States economic assistance, is experiencing a spurt of growth which recalls the American 1920's and makes contemporary American advances, for all the economy's surface affluence, seem as laggard as did Europe's after 1923.

researchers spend effort devising lists of queries which statistical samples of the population are asked to answer. It is assumed that the answers will be reasonably truthful or that the distortions will be as informative as replies which are factually true. One such study was conducted by *Time* magazine,[5] which tried to find out what kind of work and lives college seniors thought themselves likely to have fifteen years after graduation. The replies given in the middle 1950's indicated that that portion of Young America which could afford the fees at the colleges where the subjects were studying had a wholesome regard for actuality: it concentrated on the possible and kept its aspirations to itself.

For the questionnaire showed that few of those questioned expected to make great fortunes for themselves; few intended to start new enterprises of their own. All wanted the creature comforts in goodly measure—cars, houses stocked with gadgets, and the like. But happiness rather than success was their announced goal, and happiness was to be found in prompt marriage and living with a growing family among other growing families in a soot-free suburb where the only visible problems were those related to one's own personal life.

Privatism, belief that a satisfying existence is attainable only by shutting oneself up in a family of one's own as quickly as possible, seems to indicate how deeply lonely many people were and how anxious they were made by the condition of their lives. Privatism is not new, either. All the philosophic advocates of cultivating one's own garden proclaim its merit as a way of life. In the 1920's, as has been

[5] At this very moment, perhaps, some social scientist may be devising an inquiry designed to learn why people are willing to spend time filling out blanks and submitting to interviews when neither offers any tangible reward.

noted, the young abandoned concern with public life. That was prompted, at least in part, by disillusionment; the statesmen to whom they had listened proved to be clay from head to foot. But many of the generation of the 1920's dedicated their private lives to rebellion and excitement. The eagerness with which Young America of the 1950's put on the traces seemed strange indeed. Significant are the magazine articles which tell their readers how to be *acceptably* "different." The conformity in non-conformity of Bohemia in the 1920's seems to have filtered down to Suburbia. Allowing one's tastes to be directed, whether to conformity or fashionable non-conformity, may be harmless enough, yet it indicates both lack of trust in oneself, and a kind of anxiety at even the possibility of being behind—or before—the fashion and so, somehow, alone.

"A home of one's own" had long been an American ideal, as it has been an ideal of men all over the world. The need for housing was high after World War II, and the Federal government made loans for building single-family houses easy to get. Such financial incentives and the increasing unpleasantness of life in large cities stimulated a great movement out of cities onto more or less open land where a man and his family could have space, clean air, and quiet. In the suburbs he could send his children to public schools without exposing them to crowding, inferior teaching—and association with what he considered the less desirable minority groups. The move toward Suburbia seemed to entail an increasing encapsulation of experience for many Americans, and to introduce the beginnings of a new kind of social stratification. Since income generally dictates where one can live, this sorting process had always been present. But older communities have fringe areas, regions of social movement

where children of different social levels approach each
other and at least become aware of each other's existence.[6]
Contemporary suburbs are often so much of a piece, their
residents so much alike in age, income, and even type of
occupation, that, for a significant portion of his life, the
child who grows up there may be unaware that people unlike him and his parents exist.

In such an enclosed and protected environment a young
man might possibly feel free to be himself—or, as is more
likely, the pressure of homogeneity might increase his
tendency to conformism. Into such an environment, a
family might retire, "the world forgetting, by the world
forgot." Neither protection nor conformity, however, as-
sures a man of his individuality—psychotherapists tell us
many a patient from such an environment does not have a
genuine knowledge of who he is.[7]

The development of alienation between people has been
fostered by the increasing competitive pressures of life in
an industrialized world. Even involvement with another
person is sometimes felt to carry a threat to one's own psychological integrity. Since many people are no longer wholly
certain that they do constitute selves, thorough, spontaneous
involvement with others is felt to entail unbearable risk.
But inability to open out into full involvement entails other
kinds of suffering. People who fear the consequences of
involvement fear loneliness, too, and the conditions of contemporary life foster loneliness. Modern loneliness is re-

[6] Studies like *Elmtown* and *Yankee City* show how firm stratification
can continue to be even in areas where public schools have relatively
representative populations.
[7] A recent study of this problem has been made by Hendrik Ruitenbeek in the *Individual and the Crowd: A Study of Identity in America*
(New York: Nelson, 1964).

lated to isolation, of course, but it is also related to the person's inability to move outward.

Another trend, not unrelated to privatism, is exemplified by the young men and women (and not only in the United States, it must be noted) who have declared their independence of politics and particularly of political ideas. These citizens may vote, but they announce that they are voting for men, not for parties, and therefore actually not for principles. Here Young America in the 1950's was, and continues to be, supported by professional students of politics and history whose research into the details of election campaigns and legislative enactments convinced them that Americans always have been in basic agreement on all issues of public policy; when Americans thought they were dealing with real issues, they were beguiled.[8]

Indifference to larger questions in politics and general reluctance to recognize and attack social problems are not new, as reference to our earlier discussion of the decades after the Civil War will testify. Nor has this abdication of political concern meant total political indifference. As people move into smaller communities, they may become more concerned about local politics. Because the problems which arise there are more immediate and on a smaller scale, it is easier to become informed about them. Dealing with such problems—schools, building regulations, garbage disposal, for example—on a thoroughly local basis may, however, be more difficult than expected. For relatively few contemporary situations are so completely local that they can be constructively dealt with in disregard of a larger context.

[8] C. Vann Woodward has some pithy comment on this in an article for the general reader (*New York Times Book Review*, July 28, 1963, p. 1) which refers to the work being published in the professional journals.

Schools in less wealthy towns, for example, might well benefit from Federal subsidies—or might suffer from Federal interference. The issues which concern homogeneous groups like those of contemporary Suburbia also tend to focus attention on means and persons rather than on ends. Such a focus may be appropriate, at times, but concentration upon it fosters a hamperingly parochial habit of mind.

It is obvious that, except for the artist and the independent professional, most people's incomes—and the material quality of their lives—depend on achieving a good place in an organizational hierarchy. Large enterprises often use psychologically sophisticated methods of hiring and promoting employees. Personnel departments try to sort pegs and holes properly: particularly, they try to make certain that a peg once accepted will not change shape. So men allow their attitudes as well as their aptitudes to be tested, their social as well as their vocational behavior to be directed.[9] In spite of privatism, for the sake of getting and keeping jobs, the very people who most cherish their private lives tolerate a high level of intrusion upon what once would have been considered their privacy. A number of sociologists see men as getting from their leisure the sense of freedom and accomplishment that they used to derive from their work. But if employees live and work in the same small town (as more and more of them are doing, with the corporate vogue for moving white-collar operations out of large cities) and so are highly visible both to supervisors and to their competitive fellow employees, one wonders how free a man's "free" time may actually be.

But contemporary conformity is more than acquiescence

[9] A man's associates and the social aptitudes of his wife are held relevant to his qualification for promotion to higher executive rank.

under pressure; it expresses common response to the increasingly common content of experience in a mass-produced world. Where so many of the impinging stimuli are alike, reactions may well resemble each other, and doing as one's neighbor does comes spontaneously. When people are behaving like others, they feel most fully themselves. For it is then that they have a sense of belonging.

Furthermore, conformity has become a source of psychological comfort. The many contemporaries who conform because behaving like others makes them comfortable concern us in a different way from those who conform because they dare not pay the price of doing otherwise, individualists though they say they are and though they may be. These intimidated people kick against the pricks, at least in interior monologue or in the safety of conversation with their friends. They are aware of opposing some of what they comply with, and their silent rejection may at some time reach a degree of intensity where it will express itself in a useful kind of rebellion.[10] But those who conform to comfort their spirit, as it were, seem to be in search of community. They want to belong, to fit in.[11] Their community is not a shared creed; still less is it a shared residence. It is a shared way of life, economically linked to commercial or industrial bureaucracy, socially mobile in that mores and personal ties tend to shift with a man's shifting place in the hierarchy; friendly associations are almost as interchangeable as the parts of a machine. The economic link often engenders insecurity, for although personnel depart-

[10] Essays like William H. Whyte, Jr., "How to Cheat on Personality Tests," indicate that a number of people resent efforts to intrude into their psychological privacy. *See The Organization Man* (New York: Simon and Schuster, 1956).

[11] People usually find it possible to conform, but whether what they find constitutes real community is doubtful.

ments may try to make company announcements resound with team spirit and other echoes of adolescent fellowship, corporate management actually exists to maximize profits, not personal gratification. If adaptation to mobility means an increasing shallowness in personal relationships, as it appears to do, those contemporary students of society who contend that conformity for psychological soothing produces a mere counterfeit of community are justified. If the interchangeable man is the man of the future, however, the troubled social scientist may be anachronistic in his concern.

The articles of the American secular faith have not changed too much over the centuries, and paradoxes implicit in that faith continue to affect feeling, thought, and action. To be sure, about a third of all Americans are Roman Catholics nowadays, but a Church governed by the descendants of Irishmen has taken on a Puritan if not a Protestant coloring. In its dedication to the destruction of communism, the Church today proclaims its allegiance to the doctrine of private property as a natural right. And however carefully Roman Catholic spokesmen may hedge their views, their statements are rather frequently regarded by even friendly interpreters as making the objective of all social policy the moral support of the *status quo*. Getting and spending thus becomes a proper human aim. (Ironically, the Catholic community may be accepting what has been known as *the Protestant ethic* just as many Protestants may be beginning to reject it.)

The American land is settled, but Americans still live in a wilderness. That wilderness is not unpeopled nor is it limited to the Western Hemisphere. The contemporary wilderness is the post-atomic world. If men do not try to exert control over that world, the chance of there being no world to concern them is high indeed. Yet faith in the potential importance of individual action as a means of saving oneself and others from the real hell which can open beneath us is hard for the contemporary person to maintain. The man at the bench has long been a detachable part of a machine. Now, even a well-trained technician is becoming a replaceable cog. The really good administrator, according to the theories of modern universities' schools of business, is a person unencumbered by too much specific knowledge but possessed of the drives and the manipulative techniques which will enable him to keep his work force producing cheaply and his enterprise returning a profit. (This is usually termed *developing qualities of leadership*.) Yet often even the executive is aware that what is called *his* successful administration is actually the result of accumulated capital (which he neither acquired nor owns), of technical knowledge (which he does not necessarily possess), and of the shifting of prices (with which the antitrust laws forbid him to tamper).

And outside the bounds of individual relationships and economic life, the character of each man's existence depends on the movement of external events upon which, as one person, he can exert only the most tenuous kind of influence. The man who said and thought he believed Puritan doctrine was caught in a contradiction and much of his behavior indicated that the contradiction gave rise to conflict. [12] The contemporary American who says and thinks he accepts the current philosophy proclaiming the

[12] It can be argued, as we said earlier, that many people dimmed their awareness of that conflict by concentrating on making money. Many others, of course, did not experience conflict because they paid no attention to contradictions.

glories of individualism is caught in a contradiction which is almost the converse of that which his predecessors experienced. Niebuhr and other neo-Orthodox theologians accuse modern man of the sin of pride and urge that he assume a more modest posture. For impotent, he believes himself powerful. He has inherited a conviction that he can act as an individual, and should, yet his individuality is not only frustrated in a mass society, it is often regarded as inappropriate or even threatening to others. More important, where success so often goes to those who conform, readiness to conform increases. The Puritan who refused to conform when he considered conforming ungodly thought he knew God's will well enough to force others to behave as that will required. The Puritan's successor in our time often thinks non-conforming unworldly (which, in a secular society, is equivalent to being ungodly).

We have followed the American through many stages of his development, marked always by paradox. Perhaps paradox is a necessary condition of life. The existential philosophy which is currently so fashionable would say so. It is for world historians to decide whether Americans are actually more plagued by inconsistency than citizens of other countries. Here, in the hope that awareness may be the first step to freedom, we have pointed out some of the problems with which we in this country struggle and must continue to struggle.

Index